The Voice Over
Actor's Handbook

The Voice Over Actor's Handbook

How to Analyze, Interpret, and Deliver Scripts

Second Edition

JOHN BURR

Contents

Why I Wrote This Book

Try to recall a voice over performance that you thought was awesome, such as a commercial read, a documentary, a biography, or an audiobook. Didn't it make you wonder what knowledge and skills made that performance so effective?

Nearly all the voice over books I've read (and recommend in my bibliography) do a great job of describing the business, ways to get into the mood and direction of the script, approaches that give the producer what he or she wants, marketing challenges, and other issues. They also show you how to set up your own studio and get work from the internet and other sources. However, I have never read a book about voice over, stage, or film acting that examined the ways that the structure of our written language. Language dynamics affects nearly every aspect of script analysis and delivery.

This book delves into the nitty-gritty: elements of diction, dialect control, phrasing, content comprehension, parts of speech, inflection, vocabulary, context, pronunciation, and comparison/contrast, as well as how these tools apply to every script you will encounter. Developing a thorough understanding of these elements, as well as incremental control of pace, pitch, pause, volume, flow, timing, and emotional level, will transform you into a highly skilled voice over actor.

Over the course of twenty-five years of voice over coaching, it became apparent to me that a high percentage of my students did not fully understand sentence structure and grammar—and how these affect the way we read aloud.

As I listened carefully to the performances of some of the best voice over talents in the business, as well as those of stage and film actors, I began to see strong connections in how the dramatic content of the script related to the grammar fundamentals I had learned in school. On the negative side of these observations, I watched many professional actors working on stage in choice roles who lost their audience because they didn't fully understand the phrasing and structure of the lines they were trying to communicate, not to mention the basics of pace, pitch, and pause. Most of my beginning students share these shortcomings. They initially fail to grasp how to determine which words are important and which are just connective tissue or redundant, and they do not know how to apply those observations to the delivery of a script. After over twenty years of recording these observations, I have written this book. I hope it will motivate you to deeply explore the dramatic possibilities that lie within the structural dynamics of the English language.

I repeat several concepts in different contexts throughout this book. That is intentional, as they serve as reminders about principles previously introduced and discussed. They will be offered later in new situational settings that may be different from applications presented and discussed earlier in the book. This will help you to review and absorb these principles.

Most books about grammar are concerned with teaching people to *write* colorfully and correctly. This book teaches you how to *interpret* colorfully and correctly. It illustrates how each element influences the message, and it will help you better understand where and how the words in a phrase or sentence relate to one another and how to distinguish between words that should be given prominence and those that flow through without emphasis, all with the goal of helping you succeed with every script you deliver.

I realized early on in writing this book that in many cases, it would be a great challenge for the reader. You may not have learned in school all you need to know about the English language to have the tools you will need to pursue a career in script interpretation. There is a lot of linguistic information to absorb. However, even if you don't know a participle from a preposition, don't be discouraged. The examples in the book will demonstrate my points, whether you are familiar with the grammatical terms or not, and if you practice diligently, the lessons will sink in and become habit.

If you have a burning desire to be the best you can be and are willing to put in the time and effort to improve your interpretive skills, this book will serve as a ready reference source to help you achieve your goals.

Acknowledgments

No project like this is ever done by one individual. It takes many minds and hands to make it come together.

I want to thank Bradley Keville for his considerable assistance in putting all the pieces of this book together.

Special gratitude is extended to Jane Ingalls, who gave me her direct and honest critique and offered sage advice on how to make the book relevant and effective. Kudos to Rennie Carter, whose sharp editing eye made the book clearer and more concise, and to Shane Morris, who timely responded to my request to read the book and gave me his instinctive reaction to the content.

My sincere appreciation goes to my current and former students, who have functioned as my linguistic laboratory for this book. I have learned much from you all.

How to Access the Audio Segments

To access the audio files (MP3) that accompany this book, go to http://johnburrvoice.com/handbook/ and use this code: **q9B465ndr**.

Track-access numbered cues precede each chapter section of *examples* and the *practice scripts* that pair with chapter 26. Simply select the access number that corresponds with the section you want to hear. These are frequently split up into small sections so that you may repeat playback several times while you are working on them.

Here is an example: **6–15**

To explain the numbering in the example, the first number (**six**) represents the chapter. The second number (**fifteen**) represents the segment in the chapter, beginning with number **one**.

Chapter One

ATTRIBUTES OF THE VOICE OVER ACTOR

Many who aspire to be voice over talents express great concern about "the competition." They hear a couple of well-produced demos and quickly say to themselves, "I don't have a voice like that, and therefore, it is useless for me to pursue a career in voice over." This is a mistaken notion.

There are many, many successful voice over artists who succeed almost totally on the uniqueness of their sound and personality. Most producers have grown weary of the classic stentorian radio-style voice and are looking for a natural, realistic delivery, particularly from voices that have distinctive emotional traits. Some voices just naturally have a happy, bouncy, carefree quality; others may have a very dark, focused, angry, or arrogant quality, for example.

When a producer listens to a demo tape, he or she always has an immediate reaction of acceptance or rejection. This reaction also has, to a greater or lesser extent, a *subjective* element. The sound of your voice may remind the producer of someone or a type of person he or she likes or dislikes. You can do nothing about this. No matter how good any particular actor is, there is always a producer (or several) for whom he or she has little or no appeal. This, of course, is the downside.

On the upside, you are one of a kind. Revel in your uniqueness. Approach the production of your demo, your auditions, and the projects you are awarded with confidence, and rejoice in your own special self. Be who *you* are. It's all you have, and if you have talent, more often than not, it's enough.

Voice Quality

Most people who gravitate to voice over work, particularly in a transition from another career in midlife, do so because they have been told by several colleagues or friends that they "should be on radio or TV." This is generally a good sign, although until your voice and basic interpretive ability are assessed on mic by a professional producer or voice coach, you really don't have a definitive opinion from which you should move forward. Moreover, once you have one professional opinion, it's not a bad idea to get at least a couple more. Remember, a component of these opinions will be *subjective*.

Since your voice will usually be underscored by music or sound effects in the final audio or visual product, your voice should have carrying power (i.e., it should have enough of a resonant "edge" to be easily understood and theatrically effective over its underpinnings). If your characteristic sound ranges from very soft to bordering on a whisper, or if your delivery is consistently very flat, you will probably not be a good fit for voice over work.

Personality and Natural Talent

The more distinctive and outgoing your *personality* is, the better. If you are able to take a script and bring it to life with your own personal stamp of naturalness, you will probably appeal to a significant number of producers who will give you work.

Some people really bubble—really *gush* (some to nauseating excesses)—but they appeal to many people, especially ad-agency producers. They wouldn't be getting the work if they didn't. A few have a naturally dark—sometimes even macabre—side to their spoken personality that comes through on mic. Others may naturally read an informational or teaching script with great authority. Remember, this is about what comes *naturally* to you. For many voice over actors, this is only a point of departure for a broad range of emotions. This is where *talent* enters the picture. However, even people who are not naturally outgoing can learn to excel at this. This is a function of *determination*.

Reading Ability

You absolutely, positively must have a good basic ability to read and *understand* copy. This not to say that you may not have some trouble pronouncing certain proper names, technical or medical terms, foreign names or terms, and so forth. You can resolve these problems by getting the correct pronunciation from the producer or other sources and notating the script. If you cannot read sentences smoothly and naturally from fresh material, then don't even *think* about a career in this business.

Cold Reading

Here I am defining *cold reading* as the first read in a recording session after looking over the copy, not *sight-reading*.

There is some debate as to whether or not an actor's ability to read cold is significant. I believe that there are two answers to this debate: It is relatively unimportant in the production of a ten- to sixty-second radio or TV spot. In this script category, there is generally a favorable ratio between time available to perfect the script with the producer and the time it takes to *record* it, even when those involved have not gone over the script prior to the recording session. However, that ratio changes dramatically in a *narration* recording session. Because the talent usually receives the script well in advance of the recording session, there should be sufficient time to work through it so that studio time won't be wasted on repeated takes. If you can't get into the message quickly, you are going to have problems, and consequently your work will require extensive editing. This means more recording and editing time spent by the recording engineer and more studio costs to the producer. In a home studio, this will cost you only time—but sadly, often *lots* of it.

Finding Confidence

No one is confident 100 percent of the time. Some people are more naturally confident than others. If you're having a bad day for one reason or another, and you have a recording session scheduled for 3:00 p.m. that requires you to be bright-eyed and bushy-tailed, doing the session late in the day may affect your *confidence*. Under these circumstances, it's a good idea to schedule earlier in the day, when you are fresh, rested, and more likely to feel confident and positive.

However, you may naturally be easy-going, inoffensive, and accommodating instead of confrontational. You may receive a script to read that requires you to be confident to a fault—even arrogant. You must have the ability to turn this on—incrementally—to imagine that you are confident to the degree the script demands, and this projection must not be influenced by your mood or the challenges life has thrown at you on that particular day. As they say in showbiz, the show must go on. If you don't feel confident, *pretend* you do. After all, it's all about *acting*, isn't it?

Life Experience

To further our ability to fantasize according to the dictates of the script, we draw from the *experiences* of our own lives. The longer we live, the more plentiful this resource becomes. Some people lead fuller, richer, more developed lives than others. They will have a leg up in this business, as they will have a cascading fountain of experiences from which to draw. In many of the high-profile documentary and biographical

4

assignments, the lion's share of the work goes to people fifty and over, which illustrates how much producers value an actor's ability to bring the wisdom and experience of half a lifetime or more to the table.

It is also worth noting that one of the strong attractions of this business is that there is no retirement age limit. If you can do the job and do it well, you'll get work.

Imagination

Imagination is the ability to picture or imagine scenarios that are described or suggested by a given script. The more active your imagination, the better. Many scripts can bring to mind several scenarios, if you have the ability to conjure them up. You only need one to make it work. The visualization puts you squarely in the middle of the emotional drama of the script. You are *there*.

Awareness

Awareness is an aspect of experience that describes an ability to draw from nuances in life that most people are not even looking for.

Actors use their awareness to define characterizations in particular. No inflection, change in pitch, tempo, rhythm, pause, or mood goes by unnoticed by the actor who is endowed with acute awareness.

Continuing education can enhance this skill. Many fine points of life pass us by unless somewhere, somehow, someone makes us aware of them.

Imitation Skills

A close relative of awareness is the ability to imitate. It has been said that there is nothing new under the sun—that all of life is imitation. We all begin life repeating that which we see and hear from parents and family. The very first sounds we make as we try to communicate are imitative. We tell jokes about people and reproduce their characteristics. The great impersonators have developed this into an art form. We imitate personalities, accents, dialects, and even sound effects. There is a very strong visual component to this, as well.

Often, a script may be about a subject that may require a voice over actor to identify with someone who is the very antithesis of himself or herself.

Some voice over actors primarily do radio work—news, weather, sports, talk shows, and the like. Others are predominantly spokespersons. Many specialize in character voices or dialects. Only a very small percentage of people can do nearly all of the above. If you can do one of them well, you can be successful, depending on how carefully you have analyzed your market and your suitability for it, and how persistently you market yourself.

Foreign Language Skills

If you have had the benefit of extensive study in Latin, German, French, Italian, Spanish, or other languages, this will add to your ability to read copy effectively. Many otherwise competent actors have little or no foreign language skills, which thus impedes their ability to pronounce the names of foreign politicians, artists, musicians, and writers. They also might struggle with musical terms (primarily Italian), medical terms (primarily Latin), and the lexicons of sciences, law, and mathematics (Latin and Greek), for example.

As a ready example of this problem, at least 60 percent, by my estimate, of the professional narrators I have worked with have brutal difficulty pronouncing the French word *Champs Elysees*. Try it yourself. If you've had a couple of good years of French, you can probably pronounce it in your sleep.

Attention to Accuracy

Most of the time, a lot of effort goes into writing a good script; probably a lot of effort also goes into writing a bad script. In either case, as a professional, you owe it to the producer who hires you to read the script as written, faithfully to the letter. An added or subtracted word or phrase here and there will annoy the producer to distraction. Above all, be a diplomat. Ask for clarification if the script is nonsensical, grammatically incorrect, or incomplete.

Musical Ability/Training

There is some relationship between the speaking voice and the singing voice, and many singing parameters also apply to speech. They are pitch, timbre (tone), rhythm, and tempo, as well as all-important phrasing. These characteristics are not as well defined in speech as in music, but they are nonetheless noteworthy (no pun intended).

If you have a background in music, particularly singing, you will probably be at a great advantage in learning how to read scripts. The lack of musical training need not be a hindrance, however.

Ability To Control Parameters

DICTION

Good diction manifests itself by being completely and totally understood by the listener. There should be no "What did he or she say?" or "What was that word?" or "I didn't grasp it." Diction does *not* mean overpronouncing words and over articulating final consonants. Your delivery should be smooth, comfortably slow, and conversationally natural.

DIALECT CONTROL

The dialect I'm describing here refers to *regional* dialect—the kind that says to the listener, "I'm from Nayshville, Nwahlens, Bahston, Chicahgo,

7

Minnesohta, Noo Yawk," etc. If you can do any or all of these well in a script that *calls* for a regional dialect, as well as a variety of characters, you are tailor-made for that aspect of this business. Remember that you are in business to do a variety of assorted commercials and narrations, and your delivery should not be habitually tinged with one of these regional dialects. You should be reading in a straight, dialect-free American accent.

PITCH

Your ability to distinguish and identify *pitch* changes in the speech process is of paramount importance. Emotional range is conveyed more by pitch change than any other speech parameter, as is perceived *distance* from the listener. This concept is described with examples in "Understanding and Interpreting the Script."

PAUSE

Pauses create powerful drama. You must have a strong sense of where and how long to *pause* between phrases, sentences, or paragraphs. Pause also applies to an understanding of how to break up longer sentences into shorter, more dramatic events and to sense breaks between time frames, mood changes, and other dramatic shifts.

TIMBRE

As the emotional needs of the script change, so does the *timbre*, or tone, of your voice. If you are reading a promotional spot for a TV sitcom or sports event, you will need to be able to put an edge on your voice, and you will be speaking with highly charged emotion. The music under your voice will be bombastic and driving, so you will need all the carrying power you can muster.

If, however, you are doing a radio spot for a romantic French restaurant, your voice could conceivably be up close and mellow. The background could contain light café music—an accordion with a small string ensemble, for example. You must be able to adapt the timbre of your voice to accommodate these varying moods.

PACE

Pace, of course, is another word for speed. How fast or slow do we speak as we interpret a script's message? As with other parameters, we must be able to control the pace as emotional and dramatic needs dictate, and make certain that every word we utter is clear to and understood by the listener. This is also a constantly changing characteristic. Generally, in real life, the more emotionally charged a situation, the faster we speak, and we often slow down dramatically when we are making a very important point, except in automotive ads, for example. In voice over work, pace is generally slow and slower. The illusion of excitement is created mostly by *pitch change* and *timbre*.

Pace is also about keeping a consistent overall rate or tempo throughout the project.

VOLUME

Volume, like pace, is applied in small increments. Since we are working so close to the microphone, we cannot go from a near whisper to a shout as in real life. The recording equipment won't take it without distorting from the shouting. We have a working range available to us that goes approximately from soft speech to a conversational, one-on-one level. The emotional dynamics are effected primarily by pitch change and timbre, not volume.

If a producer brings in a script that requires a loud, edgy, almost shouted delivery, such as a hard-sell car commercial, the engineer will set the levels according to how loud you will read it. This level is set only for this spot; it is not set relative to anything else. Your level is simply

9

turned down so it won't distort. There is not much dynamic range to the piece; it is simply loud all the way through.

ABILITY TO VISUALIZE AND REACT

Every subject we talk about requires *visualization*. All events evoke a picture. You must be able to clarify and color this picture for yourself and the listener. For example, if you are narrating the experience of a day spent in Paris, you must be there (or have been there) yourself in your fantasy. Otherwise, how can you possibly take someone else (the listener) there? If you talk about climbing the Eiffel Tower, see yourself (and others) climbing it. Smell the rarified air as you ascend the tower. Hear the hundreds of footsteps of people coming down past you as you continue your climb to the top. When you get to the top, you take in the panorama of Paris at its most glorious. If your description continues with experiences on the ground, feel the presence of the French people and smell the aroma of freshly baked bread.

In contrast, if you are reading a World War II script describing a fierce, deadly battle, place yourself there in your mind. Soldiers fall, wounded and dying, all around you. Cannons. Rifle fire. Machine guns. Grenades. You must react to it. The listener will react with you. Live the *experience* in your mind. It's all about *empathy*—the ability to experience as your own the feelings of someone else. The best actors in the business fully understand and make use of this ability in every acting challenge they encounter.

Chapter Two

DICTION AND ARTICULATION

G ood diction is *NOT* about talking with an affectation. It *is* about *clarity*—making sure that what you say is understood while retaining a smooth, relaxed, natural feel and a delivery that is perceived as spontaneous.

To begin, let's examine the interaction of *vowels* and *consonants*:

Vowels:

> *A, e, i, o,* and *u* are the *vowels* of the alphabet. All of the *timbre*, or tone, in singing and speech is expressed in vowels.

Consonants:

> The rest of the alphabet is made up of *consonants, b, c, d, f, g, h, j, k, l, m, n, p, q, r, s, t, v, w, x,* and *z*, which, when combined with vowels, give meaning and clarity to words and form the basis for language.

Y functions primarily as a *consonant* at the beginning of a word, a *vowel* or a *consonant* in the middle of a word, and a *vowel* at the end of a word:

2–1

At beginning (consonant): *yawn, year, yogurt, yucca*

In middle (vowel): *gyroscope, hydraulic, myself, tycoon* (*eye* sound); *hypocrite, myriad, nymph, symbol* (*ih* sound)

11

In middle (consonant): *bayou, bayonet, coyote, joyous*

At ending (vowel): *carefully, photography, pity, Sotheby* (*ee* sound); *by, my, occupy, sky* (*eye* sound)

Y also functions in the manner of a consonant in the articulation of *u* sounds (*yoo*) in the interior of a word:

2–2

genuflect	lapis lazuli	ecumenical	circular
(*yoo*)	(*yoo*)	(*yoo*)	(*yoo*)

Phrases, clauses, and sentences flow smoothest when consonants and vowels alternate with one another (consonant-vowel-consonant-vowel-consonant, etc.)

2–3

"Looking out over the shoreline, I saw hundreds of migrating water birds."

This is a very smooth, descriptive, aesthetic sentence, in which the flow from vowel to consonant to vowel all the way to the end of the sentence goes unbroken. There are departures from the pattern, but they do not affect smoothness. *Looking* ends with a soft *g* but flows right into *out*. Likewise, the ending *g* in *migrating* is soft, so the movement from migrating to *water* is also smooth, since the *w* in water is not a hard consonant. The same is true for the movement from *water* to *birds*.

The goal should always be to deliver sentences with a smooth flow, as this sounds natural and comfortable to the listener.

Glottal Start

There are also situations where one word flowing into the next ends with a soft consonant, and the word into which it flows begins with a vowel. In this situation, flowing through this movement from one to the other may not sound clearly articulated. Here, we use a *glottal start* to the vowel that begins the next word.

Also known as a *glottal stop* by some speech therapists, a *glottal start* is a sound created by closing the *glottis*, which is a small opening in the larynx, and then releasing the sound in a burst of air. Some British dialects, such as Cockney (*butter* as *buh-uh*), Bristol, and Manchester, abound with glottalisms. One everyday expression that illustrates the glottal start is *uh-oh*. As with this expression, in everyday practice, the glottal start is used between *vowels* for clarity:

2–4

"Our company is committed to[ ]excellence."

"We are here to[ ]honor this man for his sacrifice."

Glottal starts on *excellence* and *honor*. Note that *honor* is pronounced as an *o* vowel.

Here's a sentence with several examples in it:

"Anyone who listens with a keen <u>ear</u> or observes with a perceptive eye can come up with amazingly fresh <u>insights</u> about human behavior."

Glottal starts on the underlined words make them stand out dramatically. If the words are read *without* the glottal starts, the drama diminishes.

Here's an example where an ending vowel to a beginning vowel may be delivered smoothly, without affecting intelligibility:

"If you ever hit m[e a]gain, it will be the last time you hit anyone."
(Note a glottal start on *anyone*, for dramatic emphasis.)

Now, here are sentences with two illustrations of where a glottal start is needed:

2–5

"Last week, I debated with myself about what car to buy, a Hond[a A]ccord or a Hyunda[i E]lantra."

"We need a commitment t[o e]xcellence."

"We are here today t[o h]onor this man."

"The smell of wisteri[a a]nd honeysuckle permeated the air."

Look for these various combinations in narrations by seasoned pros on documentary, biographical, technical, medical, and industrial narrations, on either TV or DVDs, and listen to them carefully and analytically. It is important to keep your articulation of beginning, interior, and ending consonants within the limits of a gentle delivery. Any more than this will not sound natural and comfortable to the listener.

Tongue-Twisters

One of the most popular and useful of diction exercises is the *tongue-twister*. The following is a list of original tongue-twisters—one for each letter of the alphabet, plus *PH* and *TH* words.

Some tips:

- Begin carefully, and don't rush.
- Make sure the beginning and end of each word is articulated, and don't slur words together.
- Read and repeat each phrase, clause, and sentence, slowly getting faster and faster, while maintaining clarity. If you have difficulty reading smoothly, go back and restart from your first, slowest read.

2–6

A words:
Annoying Annie ate all the apples and assuaged an avid appetite.

B words:

Billy and brother Bobby battled at Bingo. Bobby's better Bingo bothered Billy, but Billy bested both brilliantly.

C words:

Carl carefully controlled Catherine's conversations coldly. Catherine condemned Carl to the core for his cranky cut-ins.

D words:

Doug dug a deep dingy dungeon for the devil as a destination for the dastardly and devious.

E words:

Ethel eagerly eats eggs, egrets, emus, and elephants.

F words:

Familial Frieda fearlessly fried a fabulous fish feast.

G words:

Gertrude's garters garnished Gertrude's gorgeous gams.

H words:

Horrified, Harry handed Henry heavy hammerheads.

I words:

Irma's intimidating intelligence increasingly intrigued Ivan.

J words:

John Jacob Jones joined Jimmy's Junior Jumpers.

K words:

Killer kangaroos kick kung-fu klutzes to kingdom come.

L words:

Laura landed limited limelight legitimately.

M words:

Mary's marigolds made Martha's mugworts miss.

N words:
Norman knows Nellie's nausea needs nursing.

O words:
Otto offered Oliver the opportunity to order Oreos. Otto offered other options, but Oliver opted out.

P words:
Paul poisoned poor Pamela's parrotfish.

PH words:
Phyllis phoned physicians and pharmacists for phosphates.

Q words:
Quincy quizzed Queenie quietly with queer questions.

R words:
Robert razzed Rhoda repeatedly, rendering Rhoda rattled.

S words:
Susie saw Sally sneaking solo surreptitiously, so Susie suspected subterfuge.

T words:
Tommy told Tanya terrible tales today.

TH words:
Theodore thought Thatcher a thoughtless thickhead.

U words:
Unbelievingly, Ursula unpacked Ulysses's umpteenth ukulele.

V words:
At Versailles on vacation, Victor volunteered a vintage vichyssoise.

W words:
Warren worriedly watched Wally wooing Wanda. Warren wanted Wanda wickedly.

X words:

Xavier x-rayed a xylophone in Xanadu.

Y words:

Yoshi yelped "Yahoo!" at the Yiddish yachtsman.

Z words:

Zebras in zoot suits zoom zippingly, zig-zagging through zoos.

Lastly, here's a set of lyrics from W. J. Gilbert, of Gilbert and Sullivan fame, for you to exercise your diction dexterity. Follow the tips, as before.

2–7

The first from *The Mikado:*

To sit in solemn silence in a dull dark dock
In a pestilential prison with a life long lock,
Awaiting the sensation of a short sharp shock
From a cheap and chippy chopper on a big black block.
To sit in solemn silence in a pestilential prison
And awaiting the sensation
From a cheap and chippy chopper
On a big, black block.

2–8

The second from *Ruddigore:*

My eyes are fully open to my awful situation—
I shall go at once to Roderic and make him an oration.
I shall tell him I've recovered my forgotten moral senses,
And I don't care twopence-halfpenny for any consequences.
Now I do not want to perish by the sword or by the dagger,
But a martyr may indulge a little pardonable swagger,
And a word or two of compliment my vanity would flatter,
But I've got to die tomorrow, so it really doesn't matter!

2–9

The third from *H.M.S. Pinafore:*

When I was a lad I served a term
As office boy to an Attorney's firm.
I cleaned the windows and I swept the floor,
And I polished up the handle of the big front door.
I polished up that handle so carefullee
That now I am the Ruler of the Queen's Navee!
As office boy I made such a mark
That they gave me the post of a junior clerk.
I served the writs with a smile so bland,
And I copied all the letters in a big round hand—
I copied all the letters in a hand so free,
That now I am the Ruler of the Queen's Navee!

2–10

The fourth from *Pirates of Penzance:*

I am the very pattern of a modern Major-General;
I've information vegetable, animal, and mineral;
I know the Kings of England, and I quote the fights historical,
From Marathon to Waterloo, in order categorical;
I'm very well acquainted too with matters mathematical,
I understand equations, both simple and quadratical,
About binomial theorem I'm teeming with a lot o' news,
With many cheerful facts about the square of the hypotenuse.
I'm very good at integral and differential calculus,
I know the scientific names of beings animalculous,
In short, in matters vegetable, animal, and mineral,
I am the very model of a modern Major-General.

Special Considerations

PLOSIVE CONSONANTS

B, hard *c*, *d*, hard *g*, *k*, *p*, and *t* are *plosive consonants*; that is, they can push out a lot of air when pronounced. On condenser microphones (which are the microphones of choice for voice over work), a puff of air from a plosive consonant may produce a bassy "pop" in the middle of the delivery, which can be an annoying distraction.

To avoid this problem as much as possible, we use a windscreen, which may be a porous foam sleeve over the microphone, or a double windscreen inserted between the performer and the microphone. These serve to divert the puff of air from a direct line to the microphone and soften the plosive.

You can learn to deliver plosive consonants directly to the microphone without popping by practicing your delivery four or five inches in front of a burning candle. It may take many hours of practice, and you may have to relight the candle countless times, but over time you will adjust and learn to deliver plosives without blowing out the candle. Then, when you work close to a microphone, you will be able to avoid popping entirely.

Sibilance

Sibilance is a pitched hissing sound produced by some people. It occurs when the natural placement of the teeth and tongue create a whistling sound when pronouncing the soft consonants *sh* and *ch*, as well as *z*, *x*, *f*, and soft *c*.

A perfect sentence for testing one's tendencies toward or away from sibilance is "Sneaky Susie snatched Sally's soft satin shoes stealthily."

If you hear this problem in playback of your work, you can teach yourself to eliminate it by doing the following: Get a thin stick, roughly a sixteenth of an inch thick (a Popsicle or ice-cream-bar stick will do the job nicely). Insert the stick between your upper and lower front teeth. Do not bite down on it or press it on your upper or lower front teeth. Hold it so that your teeth can come together and separate freely. The idea is to put the stick gently between your teeth to create enough of a space to stop the whistling. Over time, you should be able to capture a muscle-memory sensation that enables you to keep the space created by the stick without keeping the stick itself between your teeth, thus eliminating the sibilant whistle. If you find that over time your teeth gradually come together again and you start whistling, you should be able to consciously move your teeth slightly more apart without needing to use the stick. If you can't readily do that, go back to using the stick. Over time, you should be able to avoid sibilance without the stick.

Back-to-Back Consonants

There are many articulation situations when a word ends in a certain consonant or combination and is followed by a word that *begins* with the same consonant or combination. In these situations, do not try to articulate them separately, as this will not sound smooth and natural; it will interfere with the flow of your delivery. Pronounce only one sound as a bridge between two words that end and begin with the same sound or consonant combination.

Listen to the audio tracks for the following examples of the wrong and right way to articulate these two-word combinations.

2–11

S sound to an *s* sound:
"It was a fortuitou[s s]ituation for my mother."
Pronounce only one s as a bridge between the two words.

20

St sound to an *st* sound:

"It was the heavie[st st]atue he had ever lifted."

As with the previous example, use one common st as a bridge between the two words.

Z sound to an *s* sound:

"We need to buy these clothes at a men'[s s]tore."

Pronounce the z sound on men's and immediately convert to an s on store. Do not break between the two words.

Z sound to an *sh* sound:

"We need to buy these clothes at a men'[s sh]op."

This is the same as in the previous example. Convert from z to sh without a break. Do the same conversion with the remaining examples.

Sh sound to an *sh* sound:

"Henry needed to pu[sh Sh]elley to marry him by June."

St sound to an *sh* sound:

"Alex was in time to fire the fir[st sh]ot at the bank robber."

St sound to an *s* sound:

"Alicia tried to save the la[st s]urvivor's life with CPR."

Ch sound to an *s* sound:

"He needed to tou[ch s]omething to convince himself that he was awake."

There are easier combinations using different consonants, but these are the most difficult. Just remember that when the ending consonant of the first word and the beginning consonant of the second word are pronounced identically, use only one of them as common to both words. Do not use both and break between them, as the listener will perceive the delivery as overarticulated. The object here is a flowing, natural delivery from one word to the other.

If the ending and beginning consonants are identical, morph from one to the other also without a break, per the earlier examples.

The letters *c* and *g* need special consideration, as each can be spoken as a *soft* or *hard* consonant. This has evolved from Latin and Italian.

2–12

C is *hard* when followed by an *a*, an *o*, or a *u*:

[ca]tatonic	[co]rpse	[cu]lture
(hard)	(hard)	(hard)

C is *soft* when followed by an *e* or an *i*:

[ce]lebrity	[ci]trus
(soft)	(soft)

This also applies to *c* followed by a *y*:

[cy]anide	[cy]toplasm	[cy]st
(soft)	(soft)	(soft)

G is hard when followed by an *a*, an *o*, or a *u*, as with the letter *c*:

[ga]rage	[go]pher	[gu]llible
(hard)	(hard)	(hard)

G can be *soft* or *hard* when followed by an *e*, an *i*, or a *y*:

[ge]mstone	[gi]st	[gy]rocopter
(soft)	(soft)	(soft)

[ge]t	[gi]ft	[gy]necologist
(hard)	(hard)	(hard)

The combination of *gn* can be pronounced by sounding the *g* or only the *n*:

	a[gn]ostic	i[gn]orant	[gn]aw	[gn]ome
Pronounce as:	*gn*	*gn*	*n*	*n*

Special Considerations

THE ARTICLE *A*

A significant number of my students over the years were never taught that the article *a* should be pronounced as *a* in America. Some of my older students who read from the *Dick and Jane* readers were taught to read the *a* as in *date* only. Those same people continue to pronounce it the same way as adults. Unfortunately, Dick and Jane continue to live on in derivative books with new titles.

In fact, the correct pronunciation is always as *a* in [A]meric[a].

THE ARTICLE *THE*

In certain regions of the United States, particularly in the South, people habitually pronounce this article as *thuh*: thuh apple, thuh pear, thuh orange, or thuh pineapple.

Most of my students who have come to me with this habit have been surprised to learn that this is incorrect. In fact, the correct situational approach to voicing *the* goes like this: Pronounce it as *thuh* before a word that begins with a *consonant* and as *thee* before a word that begins with a *vowel*.

2–13

Before a *consonant*: *thuh* pear, *thuh* pineapple, *thuh* banana

Before a *vowel*: *thee* apple, *thee* orange, *thee* avocado

For those who have always had this problem, changing the habit will be very difficult, but it is doable if you are willing to put in the time and effort to correct it.

Contractions

2–14

Typical contractions are *didn't, couldn't, wouldn't, shouldn't,* and *mustn't.*

Unfortunately, many people have learned them as *dident, couldent, wouldent, shouldent,* and *mussent.*

Do *not* voice a *vowel* on the contraction. Voice it as you see it: did-(nt), could-(nt), would-(nt), should-(nt), and must-(nt). The *nt* is a *throwaway*—pitched low with no emphasis. You must also *connect* the contraction to the first word. Don't *pause* between the two. When you say the first syllable, your tongue sits against the roof of your mouth at the end of the syllable. If you pronounce the contractions as *dident, couldent, wouldn't, shouldent,* and *mussent,* your tongue will drop away from the roof of your mouth and back again as you pronounce the *ent.* (It will stay away from the roof of the mouth on *muss.* To say it properly as a contraction, leave your tongue against the roof of your mouth as you pronounce the second syllable: *did-n't, could-n't, would-n't, should-n't, must-n't.* Try it.

Mispronounced Words

There is an entire chapter in this book devoted to mispronounced words, and you should read it very carefully. You may be surprised by many of them. The more words you know and pronounce correctly, the more your client will appreciate and respect your study and mastery of these elements.

Finally, deliver your material in a slow, smooth, moderately soft, yet clearly intelligible style, as if you're talking to a person who is fairly new to the English language. No matter what kind of script you're delivering, if the listener doesn't understand the words, all your other efforts will have been in vain.

Chapter Three
MOOD AND EMOTION

When analyzing a new script, one of your first considerations should be the overall *tone* and *mood* it evokes. Is it a breathtaking look at scenic views, an angry reaction to a social injustice, the joy of possessing the car of your dreams, a despondent observation of poverty in Africa, a you-are-there reenactment of a wartime battle, a sad reminiscence of rioting in the streets, or a detailed, informational description of a technical or medical procedure? These are but a few of the varied subjects you will encounter, and as I'm sure you can understand, they suggest a wide variety of emotional treatments.

As you study a script, try to develop an attitude and a mood appropriate to the message. The emotional possibilities are endless. Is it a serious piece? Does it require a great deal of focus? Or is it a very casual, off-the-cuff, spontaneous-sounding piece? Does it make a lot of emphatic points or illustrations? Is it friendly? Familiar?

If it is a teaching or informational vehicle, assume that you know everything about the subject and that the listener knows nothing. This will never be entirely the case, but assume it anyway. Put yourself on a pedestal. Take on an air of supreme confidence. You are the expert, the authority. You have just come down from the mountain with tablets of wisdom in hand. (Remember, this is all *fantasy!*)

If there is one adjective you don't want applied to your delivery of a script, it is *ordinary*. It is vital that you milk every emotion *that is appropriate to the script you are reading.* If your listeners perceive that you are delivering with inappropriate, underdone, or overdone emotion, you will lose them in a heartbeat.

At first, I suggest that you diligently try to *overdo* all the emotional content that you perceive in the script. Even if it's too much at times, it's a good exercise, because this approach compels you to use emotions that you may have subdued all your life in the reading-aloud process. Left alone, the reticence, shyness, and fear of performance that you developed during school reading classes will remain. You must break away from this syndrome if you are going to come across as believable. Producers hire professional voice over actors because they know that scripts will be brought to life and made special by the actors' talents.

Smiling

Telephone solicitors are often trained to talk with you while watching themselves in a mirror. In this way, they can constantly check themselves to be sure that they're *smiling.* Can you hear a smile on people's faces when they speak to you? Absolutely. It is also very true of other emotions. I constantly tell my students that I want to see the mood of the script on their faces.

What You Can Do

Make working in front of a mirror a part of your practice regimen. Go to extremes of emotion. Experiment. Record it all, and listen to the results. You can become your own best judge of how much is enough, how much is too much, and how much is too little. In the early stages of this process, it's best to work one-on-one with a good coach to make sure that you're on the right track. You can also record commercials and narrations performed by people whose work you admire. After

26

recording, transcribe the content to give you a working script. Then listen to several playbacks and make notes of your observations. Try it yourself, record it, and listen back. Pay particular attention to how *genuine* you sound. Are you on the same emotional track that you're hearing from the performance you recorded off the air? This can be a long and frustrating process, so you must be patient. Don't expect immediate results. You will get better by increments. *Variation* is what you're after. The more varied emotions you can muster, the better. Also focus on how you incrementally *control* those emotions. The benefits you derive from these experiences can also increase the variety and amount of work available to you when you market yourself.

Chapter Four
BREATH CONTROL

Most breath-control problems stem from a lack of understanding of phrasing, especially from overlooking *pauses* that offer the opportunity to take in a breath. Others are caused by simply delivering at too high a volume or not staying *relaxed*. *Anxiety* is the mortal enemy of breath control.

Pauses give us obvious openings to breathe and, if the pause is a long one, a chance to grab a *big* breath. Most long sentences can be broken up into several shorter phrases or clauses that can stand alone (see chapters on phrasing) and can therefore offer many breathing opportunities. Mark them when prepping your script.

A word about loud delivery: stage actors (as mentioned in a previous chapter) as well as amateurs who are new to voice over often project the message as they would on stage. This is a surefire way to run out of breath. Delivering at a comfortable, relaxed, conversational level will conserve your breath in a way that may surprise you.

You should breathe *in*, in preparation for the *next* phrase. There should always be some follow-through at the end of every phrase that immediately precedes a pause.

Keep your breathing relaxed, and try not to overdo the intake. Don't rush it, either. I have heard many broadcasters (mostly from reading too fast) take short, quick gasps for breath that are frequently quite audible. The use of electronic compression often exacerbates this phenomenon. Easy does it. Try to *pitch* the breath as low as you can by making the opening in the back of your throat as wide as comfortably possible.

One way that you can build up your breathing stamina is to take a script—*any* script—and read it in an easy, relaxed, but expressive manner, all while *eliminating* every *pause*. The idea is to take a comfortable breath in the beginning and go as far into the script as you can without taking another breath. Try using the same script for a few days for this exercise. Each time you read it aloud, mark how far into the script you ran out of breath. The next time you do it, try to go a word or two or three further. Over time, you will be amazed at how far you can go without a breath. When I first started this myself, I could only do two to two and a half lines. After working on it for several months, I was able to do fourteen to sixteen lines. Many of my students have achieved similar results.

Here is another exercise that will increase your breathing capacity, as well as relax you:

Take a quick deep breath and let the air out immediately, using no resistance. In—one, two. Out—three, four. Do this a few times with thirty to sixty relaxed seconds in between so that you don't hyperventilate.

Then take a quick deep breath in as before, with your body relaxed, and instead of letting out the air on a count of two, immediately after you breathe in, purse your lips as if you were going to whistle a very high note. This will immediately create resistance to the air expelling outward, allowing it to escape very gradually. It is very important that your body stay relaxed, so the only resistance to the expelling air is your pursed lips, not your diaphragm. Let the air out, and continue to push it out until you can't stand it any longer. Then breathe in normally to relieve the discomfort. This drives endorphins right to the brain, and it will relax you. (Don't do it repeatedly, or you may hyperventilate and faint.)

Doing one of these just before you do a take is a great way to ward off anxiety. Do the exercise once as just described. Then do another, but this time, instead of breathing normally after pushing the breath out, make the next breath intake the *preparatory* intake for the first line of the script you're delivering. You can also use this in the previous exercise that eliminates all the pauses.

What you are doing here is substituting the resistance of your pursed lips with the resistance created by your vibrating vocal cords. Keep your body relaxed. Let it operate as a bellows. The air is sucked in quickly and let out very slowly. *How* slowly will determine how many lines you are able to deliver without running out of breath.

If you do enough of these exercises and do them as part of your practice regimen, you will be pleasantly surprised at how efficient your breathing will become. Be sure to make the intake as quiet as possible. Keep your throat open.

Chapter Five
PACE CONTROL

Diction

Your delivery should be smooth, comfortably slow, and conversationally natural. This means paying attention to every *word* and every *syllable* in every word, so you must give every word and every syllable its *time value*. I've heard students rush through prepositional phrases such as "In the middle of the night," which came out as "'nth'middlo'th'night," or "There are other considerations you need to keep in mind," which was said as "Therotherconsiderationsy'needt'keepinmind." There are many, many examples like these.

At least 75 percent of my beginning students read or talk too fast. Most people don't have a clue that they're doing it. This is one good reason for recording and playing back virtually every script you incorporate into your practice routine.

Pace is also such a strong component of diction that it is worthy of discussion as a topic of its own. You must think of every word as an individual word, pronounced clearly, but connected at the same time with all the other words that precede or follow it. Be slow and smooth, but carefully give each word and syllable the time it needs to be thoroughly understood.

Narrations should generally be delivered in a calm, slow, smooth, natural, focused, caring manner, with an emphasis on *slow*. This doesn't mean draggy and ponderous, but *purposeful* and *intense.*

To help you keep your pace slow and smooth, try to pretend that you are talking to a person who doesn't understand English very well, one who is relatively new to the language. Remember also that in real life, when people are very passionate about something, they slow down considerably when they talk about it; scolding a child, explaining a technical or scientific concept, showing off a new car to friends, or expounding on a belief system are but a few examples.

Note also that when you come to the end of a script, the last line—specifically the last two or three words—almost always slow down progressively. I recommend that you deliver these last words while thinking *slow, slower*, and *slowest.* This treatment gives finality and definition to the ending, which most often builds to a climax and is usually punctuated by a music build underneath it as well as a final flourish after the last word of the narration. This also happens in a buildup to a documentary or biographical title near the *beginning* of a script.

5–1

1. The last paragraph of a script about the atom bomb: "As the scientists at Los Alamos reflected on that historic day of the first explosion of the bomb, they knew the world was a changed place and that there would be no turning back." *no* (slow) *turning* (slower) *back* (slowest)

2. The last paragraph of a script about a preschool: "As you contemplate your child's early development,

consider our learning environment and how your child could benefit from it. By pursuing his or her individual interests in a Montessori school classroom, your child will gain an early enthusiasm for learning, which is the key to a continuing education throughout life."
education (slow) *throughout* (slower) *life* (slowest)

3. The last paragraph of a script about the elderly generation robbing the future of the young: "The risk of inflation scares our politicians into a reluctance to jump-start the economy with a fiscal stimulus, because it is perceived as a threat to retirement savings for seniors. Further, Congress refuses to approve job-creating infrastructure projects because they will have to be paid for with more taxes, which are almost universally opposed by seniors. It seems unseemly that in its efforts to care for the old, America is jeopardizing the quality of life for its coming generations."
its (slow) *coming* (slower) *generations* (slowest)

4. The long build to a company name that is the subject of a script: "There are many storied descriptions of companies who have risen from the ashes to make great strides in their industries. Ours is of a company whose creation and growth have surpassed almost all others in its field. The name is Holloway."
name (slow) *is* (slower) *Holloway* (slowest)

5. The dramatic conclusion of a paragraph about extinction: "From the accelerated extinctions of the dodo and the passenger pigeon to the many threatened species of today, the living creatures of the world are in danger. They are engaged in a desperate struggle for survival."
struggle (slow) *for* (slower) *survival* (slowest)

Keep in mind that all of this is meant to build or enhance the *drama*.

A word about commercials that exude excitement: when underpinned by appropriate music, they sound frenetically fast. Listen carefully. The mood is exciting. The animation may be extreme. The *speed* of the delivery is *not*.

5–2

1. "This week, at Brandywine <u>Toyota</u>, we're having a sale that will blow you <u>away</u>!"

2. "Don't <u>miss</u> this one-time opportunity to save a <u>bundle</u>!"

3. "Two <u>sandwiches</u> for the price of <u>one</u>, tomorrow <u>only</u>, at Klotz's <u>Deli</u>!"

4. "Hey kids, look what <u>I've</u> got—your very own <u>Mumsy</u> Doll! She's got real plastic <u>surgery</u> scars, just like <u>real</u> Mumsies."

5. "If you love to dance, you'll move your feet <u>big</u> time—at the Danceaway <u>Ballroom</u>, every Saturday <u>night</u>."

Listen to a wide variety of top talents on radio and television, and make every effort to observe how they handle and control *pace*.

Chapter Six
Pitch Control

Another important conveyor of mood and emotion is *pitch*. In my evaluation sessions, many of my students exhibit misconceptions about how pitch works in script delivery. They pitch up where they should pitch down and vice versa, or they don't pitch up or down *enough*.

Let's address some fundamental concepts about pitch. Pitching way up at the end of a sentence conveys a question. "Is that person standing over there your guest?" *Guest* goes up and *stays* up. On the other hand, a rhetorical question ends in a statement. "Well, now, what do you think of *that*?" or, "What are we going to *do* about this?" The pitch is raised on the italicized words only slightly to give the sentence the feel of a statement, not a question. As for all other phrases and clauses, they are delivered as pure statements, one after the other (see "Read vs. Talk"), as this is the way most people *talk* in everyday spontaneous conversation. These statements end with a *down* inflection, or a low pitch, which gives the endings a sense of *finality*.

6–1

1. "I am fed up with politics."
2. "You will get nothing from me."

3. "You are my <u>friend</u> and will <u>always</u> be my friend."
   (Two statements, delivered with a pause between them.)

4. "No city in the world compares with <u>Paris</u>."

5. "This is the <u>end</u>."

Animation is all about pitch variation. If a script is delivered with a lot of animation, the pitch goes up and down, often to extremes. If it's delivered with less animation, as in more subtle, nuanced scripts (particularly most narrations), there is far less pitch variation. Cartoons, children's stories, commercials aimed at children, and hard-sell car commercials contain a lot of pitch variation, for example. It is very important that you understand these extremes and everything in between them, as your interpretation will depend on this understanding and application.

The following exercises contain a variety of animation implications. Listen carefully to the renditions on the audio examples, then do them yourself, record them, and play them back. They begin with very little pitch change, then gradually go to extremes. You should find it useful to *imitate* the pitch changes.

6–2

1. "My best friend <u>died</u> last week." (somber, low-key)

2. "It's nice to <u>meet</u> you." (everyday pleasantry)

3. "I <u>love</u> your new car." (mild, sincere enthusiasm)

4. "I'm going to <u>Hawaii</u> next week." (conversational exuberance)

5. "What a fantastic <u>view</u>!" (enthusiastic reaction)

6. "Unwrap one of our delicious chocolate <u>truffles</u>, and therein lies <u>paradise</u>." (wishful fantasy)

7. "Wow! It sure doesn't taste like plain <u>ice</u> cream!" (bright-eyed, bushy-tailed enthusiasm)

8. "Buy it now! At your local <u>Hyundai</u> dealer! (hard-sell command)

You can even take a phrase such as, "Oh, isn't that interesting?" (a *rhetorical* question delivered as a statement) and begin with a low-key delivery. Then build the animation gradually over several reads, until the last version is over the top. Listen to how it's done on the audio segments.

The way we handle pitch change can also convey a sense of perceived *distance* for the listener. There is a reference to this phenomenon in the chapter "Understanding and Interpreting the Script." Remember that *pitch*, along with *timbre*, does more to convey emotion and emotional range than any other parameter.

Key

Key is a musical term that describes an overall level of *pitch*. Unlike pitch, which changes continuously in a sentence, paragraph, and entire piece, key is the *general* area of pitch that centers on the highs and lows of an entire script. Key is routinely specified as *high*, *medium*, or *low*.

To clarify, picture a piano keyboard. It begins with the A key on the bass (left) side of the piano and moves up the scale by steps to a full octave: A, B, C, D, E, F, G. Then it continues upward by octaves until it reaches the last, and highest, key, C, at the end of the right side of the keyboard. What is referred to as *middle C* is almost at the center of the piano. The vocal center of most *men's* voices will be within the two octaves below middle C. For most *women*, the vocal center is usually two octaves above it.

A high key is used for a script that is joyous, fun, and celebratory—in other words, one involving excitement. It can also be used to convey fear, stress, rage, or similar emotional intensity. A middle key is used for narration scripts and spots that are descriptive or that impart

37

unenhanced information. A low key correlates with dark emotions: sorrow, depression, illness, death, pity, and the like, as well as romance or seduction.

6–3

High-Key Range

1. "Leave me alone! I don't want anything to do with you! You and I are through! Get lost!"

2. "Help me! I'm trapped and I can't get out! I can't breathe! Somebody help me!"

3. "You are not leaving here until you apologize to our neighbor for breaking his window."

4. "This weekend at Hadley Toyota, we're having a sale that will blow your mind! Get a Camry SE for $209 a month, with no money down!"

5. "The fuzzy little rabbit hopped over the meadow, followed by all the other fuzzy little rabbits."

6. "This is the best hamburger I ever tasted! Wow! I want another one!"

7. "Come to Hawaii, and experience the trip of a lifetime! Whatever island you choose for your stay, you won't be disappointed!"

8. "I feel good. I want the whole world to know how good I feel. Things are definitely looking up."

9. "The intensity of the pain in his head was too much to bear. In a desperate moment, he tried to take his life, but his best friend stopped him."

10. "Give her the Valentine's gift of a lifetime. Take her to Paris. Fares have never been more affordable than now."

6–4

Middle-Key Range

1. "His life in the small town where he grew up played a significant role in shaping his character."

2. "Please do not stand in front of the elevator door when it opens, to allow passage for people exiting the elevator."

3. "The Supreme Court today voted five to four to allow corporations to refuse service to customers whom they perceived to be same-sex couples."

4. "I am calling to confirm my reservation on Flight 602, leaving at 8:30 a.m. for LA International Airport. The name is Ronald Harris."

5. "They were disappointed in the results of the election, as they were hoping for a change in the political climate."

6. "Jenny and her husband decided to go to a movie instead of the neighbor's party."

7. "Follow these instructions, and you will protect yourself against unwanted or unsolicited calls."

8. "Happy birthday. We wish we were there to celebrate it with you. We miss you and Rob very much."

9. "He tried to help her, but he realized that there was nothing he could do. If she couldn't help herself, he surmised, no one could help her."

10. "I got in my car, drove downtown, did some shopping, and went to a movie. When the movie let out, I went out for a hamburger. Then I came home and went to bed early."

6–5

Low-Key Range

1. "No one means more to me than you. I've loved you all my life. I will always love you. You are my best friend and soul mate."

2. "I owe you an apology. I hurt you, and I'm sincerely sorry. What can I do to make it up to you? I want us to be friends again."

3. "The solemn little group carried the casket down the aisle toward the altar. Members of the congregation watched, teary-eyed, as they listened to the organ playing the funeral dirge."

4. "It had been over three years since I last saw my grandfather. When I arrived at the nursing home, I went into his room, not knowing what to expect. As I had feared, he looked emaciated and feeble. I knew the end was near."

5. "He was sorry that he had lost his temper at the storekeeper. He now knew that he was to blame for the argument."

6. "The little dog was lonely. He had been taken from his mother and moved to the animal shelter, where he was put in a small cage by himself."

7. "I'm not feeling like myself. My aches and pains are getting worse. I find myself short of breath going up stairs. Old age is no fun."

8. "He looked intensely troubled. Nora had seen that look before. She was very worried about him. She put her arm around him, and he broke down, sobbing, for several minutes."

9. "I'm disappointed in you. Apparently, I expected more than you were willing to give. You don't seem to want or need my respect or anyone else's for that matter."

10. "Hundreds of protesters were shot by the guard troops and left to die in the streets. No one would come to their aid."

Note that in each category of key, the overall pitch changes, up or down, with each example. So instead of high, medium, or low, a single example might be *medium-high* or *medium-low*, for instance, within the range of medium key. These mostly occur as *incremental* key changes from one script to another, often barely perceptible, as you move down the emotional scale from high to medium to low.

Chapter Seven
PHRASING: THE ART OF THE PAUSE

Understanding where to connect and where to separate words confounds all but the most polished voice actors. The answers almost always lie in the message itself, but you must learn what to look for in order to find them.

Consider the following sentence in two versions—identical but for the comma in the second version, which changes its meaning altogether.

7–1

"I can't help you to be <u>honest</u>."

"I can't <u>help</u> you, to be <u>honest</u>."

Here's another:

"Joe spent his summer doing light <u>housekeeping</u>."

"Joe spent his summer doing <u>lighthouse</u> keeping."

These are obvious examples of how changes in connection between words alter the meaning.

Since we're talking about connecting, we must also look at where we *separate*. Within most longer sentences lie smaller sentences that will function as dramatic entities on their own. Look for the possibilities.

Remember, in verbal communication, *one word* can be a dramatic sentence. If you are outdoors with a companion and one of you sees a deer coming out of the woods, the words spoken probably won't be "Oh, look, there's a deer coming out of the woods!" They will probably be "A *deer*!" If you consider how people talk to one another, *that* is a *sentence*. In how many nature films have you heard the narrator begin with "The hippopotamus…" or "The elephant…" or "The rhino…" and so on? If you can point to a heightened emotion from any word or combination thereof, do it.

7–2

Here are some examples:

"[Welcome] to Hyatt Hotels."

"[Norman] was a bad little boy."

"[Thomas Jefferson] was one of our most well-read presidents."

"[Solder] is a metal alloy."

"Emperor of France, [Napoleon] has been celebrated and demonized for his successes and failures."

"[Fortunately], you can do something about tuberculosis."

Within longer sentences lie shorter sentences, which I call *events*. Each of these events carries its own drama in the way that a person would speak it in ordinary conversation, usually in short statements. Here are several examples. Listen to them on the audio both as a straight-through read and then as individual, declarative (statement) events. Then try them yourself, record them, and play back the results. The declarative events are bracketed within the sentences:

7–3

"[He was picked out of a police lineup], [and interrogated about a kidnapping and rape]."

"[As these forces interact to <u>change</u> how business is conducted] [there is one <u>source</u>] [to whom businesses can <u>turn</u>] [for the <u>answers</u> to their <u>problems</u>]."

"[The best <u>cooks</u> know there's always one <u>ingredient</u>] [that makes a great <u>dish</u>]."

Observe the small sentences lying within this radio script:

"[A long <u>time</u> ago] [we launched the concept of providing unsurpassed <u>service</u>] [and individual <u>attention</u>] [to owners of one of the best luxury cars in the <u>world</u>]. [Much has <u>changed</u> since that time] [but <u>today</u>] [your choice of a dealer from whom you'll buy a <u>Lexus</u>] [is simply <u>them</u>] [or <u>us</u>]. [The Lerner <u>Lexus</u> Center]."

For dramatic effect, break after a verb. If the adverb following and modifying it is followed by another phrase, *pause* before that phrase:

"[Alice <u>wept</u>] [unco<u>ntrol</u>lably]."

"[He was unable to walk or <u>stand</u>] [without ass<u>ist</u>ance]."

This works only when the emotion in the message is intense. In a more ordinary situation, a break or emphasis is not necessary:

"David read <u>studiously</u> every <u>day</u>."

Now more about connecting. Here are a couple of basic rules:

Don't break between a subject and verb or a verb and its object:

"In the middle of an intense 7th <u>inning</u>, the left <u>fielder</u> (subject) finally hit (verb) a home <u>run</u> (object)."

"The dying <u>man</u> (subject) let out (verb) a <u>death</u> rattle (object) before breathing his last <u>breath</u>."

Always break between two clauses, whether dependent or independent, as each clause is an *event*:

"I'm telling you, he is headed for <u>trouble</u>." (Preceding independent clause)

"While waiting for the train to arrive, Larry stored his luggage in a locker." (Preceding dependent clause)

Opening Statements

Many scripts begin with strong opening statements, which need to be stated emphatically and followed by a short pause, for dramatic effect.

7–4

"<u>How life began</u> (pause) is a concept that has challenged man's thinking for centuries."

"<u>The inner workings of big banks</u> (pause) have, and continue to be, kept secret from the general public."

"[<u>Ancient Egypt's antiquities</u>] (pause) still fascinate collectors all over the world."

"[<u>You Are Not Alone</u>] (pause) by Oliver Odom, now at your favorite bookstore."

"[The book <u>Leonard Bernstein</u>] (pause) is about a musical life well-lived, as pianist, composer, and conductor."

Prepositional Phrases

Various *ending* prepositional phrases can often be preceded by a breathing pause or a nonbreathing pause. The break often sets a prepositional phrase as an add-on or afterthought. Here the pauses are most often minimal.

7–5

"['What do you <u>do</u>?'] is usually the first question we ask (pause) [upon meeting a new acquaintance]."

"[Researchers] began to track specific mental illnesses (pause) [between 1994 and 2006]."

"[Many of his shipmates were killed in an explosion aboard ship] (pause) [at the Port of Los Angeles] (pause) [in 1943]." (Two in a row.)

"[The presidency of Ulysses S. Grant] was blighted by scandal (pause) [during a time of racial and social conflict in America.]"

It generally makes sense to pause after an event (subject/verb or subject/verb/object) that precedes a prepositional phrase, as long as it is not a *modifying* phrase (which would extend the *destination*), but rather a *setting* (time and/or place).

7–6

Here are examples where the preposition *leads* the sentence:

"[With one sweeping gesture,] (pause) the accused dismissed his detractors."

"[In an atmosphere of true friendship,] (pause) he felt comfortable at last."

"[In the beginning,] (pause) their relationship was very close and loving."

"[In the Constitution,] (pause) God makes almost no appearance, except in the phrase [in the Year of Our Lord 1787.]"

Settings

Prepositional phrases can also lead into a sentence as *settings*. Settings refer to time or place. They may appear anywhere in the sentence, but usually at its beginning. In every case, a setting should be stated as a strong declaration *with an ending of its own* (i.e., a sentence all by itself). This applies to *every element* of a setting.

7–7

"[In the middle of the night], (pause) strange events began to unfold." (Prepositional phrase refers to *time*.)

"[Last night], my wife and I went to see a play." (*Time*)

"[On October 23], [at three o'clock in the morning], a fire started [in the basement of City Hall]." (Both settings represent *time*.)

"[On the fourteenth day of December], (pause) [at three o'clock in the afternoon], (pause) a large explosion was heard [throughout the city]." Here, each phrase represents *time*.

"[At the beginning of the fourteenth century], (pause) [in northern Italy], (pause) the artistic influences of the earlier century began to evolve into something entirely new and different." (One pause after each. In this case, the first prepositional phrase represents *time*; the second represents *place*.)

"[Last Wednesday], (pause) [on a beautiful, sunny day in Boston], we went to see our best friend's new house." (The first two settings represent *time*; the third, *place*.)

The following example is typical of many corporate video/film scripts. A sequence of events in different time frames unfolds—first a history of the company, then a rundown of accomplishments past and present, and finally a projection of future goals and accomplishments.

"[Years ago], Company X was working on groundbreaking research. [Today], that research has paid off. [Tomorrow], [we look to worldwide expansion], as our company continues on its path to success." (All represent *time*.)

The settings in this example are only a sentence apart, for purposes of illustration. In most situations such as this, they will be *paragraphs* apart.

Here are other examples of settings appearing in different locations in the sentence:

7–8

"The spirit of the people is evident [in every city and every town]." (*Place*) (This flows smoothly with no pause.)

"And that's the way it was (pause) [in Bemidji, Minnesota] (pause) [on July 4, 2000]." (*Place* and *time*)

"Trade your hotel room for a beautiful suite (pause) [at the new Executive Suites Hotel]." (*Place*)

"[Here], (pause) [on September 17, 1862], (pause) over 22,000 Union and Confederate soldiers perished." (*Place* and *time*)

"There are thousands of Greek Revival houses [all over America] (*place*), (pause) and nowhere are they more prevalent [than in New Orleans]." (*Place*)

"You can encounter bears [just about anywhere in Alaska]—[from the Porcupine River, (pause) across the Brooks Range, (pause) to the Beaufort Sea]." (All are *place*.)

A setting "sets up" the story, hence the term <u>setting</u>. If the listener is expected to share the fantasy with you, then take him or her there by placing heavy emphasis on *time* and *place*. Getting back to prepositional phrases as afterthoughts, note that *non*prepositional phrases are set off by pauses in a similar manner:

7–9

"Poor man's philanthropist Adam Brown donated more than 180,000 dollars over his lifetime."

"Even though these foreign-aid administrators seem dedicated to the fight against hunger, (pause) [they would face unemployment] (pause) [were hunger actually eliminated]."

"More than thirty new or resurgent diseases have been identified in the last forty years, (pause) [the sort of short-term growth which many experts say has not happened since people began settling in cities]."

"It is time to seriously examine man's treatment of nonhuman animals, (pause) [if only for the consideration of human health]."

Dependent and Independent Clauses

As was stated earlier, try to think of short, simple sentences when you deliver a script. I call them *events*. If, however, these events are part of a longer sentence, we need to think in terms of *clauses*. Clauses contain a subject and a verb, while phrases do not. An *independent* clause is independent because it can function on its own as a complete sentence. A *dependent* clause is dependent because it secondarily combines with an independent clause. It is *subordinate*.

7–10

Here is an example of both kinds of clauses in one sentence:

"Harry showed me the new Mercedes that he had bought the day before yesterday."

Which line can stand alone?

1. "Harry showed me the new Mercedes."

2. "That he had bought the day before yesterday."

The independent clause is "Harry showed me the new Mercedes."

"That he had bought the day before yesterday" has a subject (*he*) and a verb (*bought*), but it does not function as a complete sentence. Rather, it's a dependent clause that in this case further *describes* the Mercedes and could be considered an *adjective clause*. The clause is introduced by the relative pronoun *that*, which, in some cases, can even be eliminated but is implied, as in the following:

> "Harry showed me the new Mercedes he had bought the day before yesterday."

Even though *that* is eliminated, it is *implied*.

The important point to remember about dependent clauses such as this is that when they begin with a real or implied relative pronoun (*that*, *who*, or *which*), the entire sentence flows smoothly from beginning to end, without a pause.

7–11

Here are other examples:

using *who*:

> "Jane tried to find out who spread the vicious rumors about her and Jack."

using *whom* (the *object* form of who):

> "The woman of whom I spoke to you yesterday recovered from her accident."

using *whose* (the possessive form of who):

> "The man whose identity was stolen was finally able to access his bank account."

using *which*:

> "The book to which I refer is a very old book."

Independent Clauses

A compound sentence—two independent clauses separated by a conjunction—virtually *always* requires a pause before the conjunction.

7–12

"[Her manner often disturbed him], (pause) [but in spite of it, he continued to escort her to special events.]"

"[Joe thought the game would be close], (pause) [but to his surprise, the home team won the game by a landslide.]"

"[We direct our generosity to crises of health and hunger], (pause) [but our aid must also incentivize private enterprise.]"

"[Few Americans know that Genesis is the first book of the Bible], (pause) [and only one-third know that the Sermon on the Mount was delivered by Jesus.]"

"[In the last ten years], (prepositional phrase pause) [Americans have elected low prices over quality in their purchases], (pause) [but animals aren't goods that can be jockeyed to achieve lower costs for food.]"

Now let's consider a combination of independent and dependent clauses where the dependent clause begins with a linking *conjunction* and *leads* the sentence:

7–13

"[When Tom saw Maria again after so many years,] (pause) [he was astounded at how strikingly beautiful she was.]"

Here a pause is needed to set off the dependent clause.

Other examples:

"[Because the sermon was so long,] (pause) [it made no difference that the other elements of the service went by quickly.]"

"[After the battle had diminished,] (pause) [medics began the grueling task of sorting out the wounded from the dead.]"

"[Until you change your mind about Henry,] (pause) [don't expect any sympathy from me.]"

"[Although I get along with her at work,] (pause) [she is not a nice person.]"

Note also that in most cases, the dependent and independent clause can be reversed, as in the last of the previous examples:

"[She is not a nice person], (pause) [although I get along with her at work.]" (*Reversed*)

The linking conjunctions to look for in these situations are *after*, *although*, *as*, *because*, *before*, *if*, *since*, *unless*, *until*, *when*, and *while*. A pause before the conjunction is almost always needed to effectively deliver such sentences, no matter whether the dependent or the independent clause comes first. Remember that we are talking about the dramatic effectiveness of the *spoken* word, not the correctness of the written word.

Participial Phrases

Participial phrases have verbs but not subjects. They can also be descriptive and act as adjectives. Depending on the construction of the sentence, they may or may not require pauses. In general, if they are set off by *commas*, they need a pause.

7–14

Here are examples of both approaches:

"[Waiting in their foxholes,] (pause) [the soldiers prepared for the imminent invasion.]"

"[Shouting angrily at the politicians in the chamber,] (pause) [the union organizers protested the hostile decision.]"

"The money lost in the stock market was all he had." (no pause)

"All of the time spent in the classroom was of no use to her now." (no pause)

Commas

You are almost always safe in pausing where you see a comma, as it is the most commonly used punctuation device to separate words, phrases, and clauses. There are exceptions, however, and you need to be aware of them. *In some cases, commas are eliminated for a spoken line, even though they may be correct for the written line, for the simple reason that they don't sound natural when spoken as punctuated.*

7–15

Here are several examples. As written:

> "It is probable, however, that they would have disapproved of his views on religion."

As delivered:

> "It is probable however, (no pause at first comma) that they would have disapproved of his views on religion."

As written:

> "Women, on the other hand, show no effects from this phenomenon."

As delivered:

> "Women on the other hand, (no pause at first comma) show no effects from this phenomenon."

As written:

> "Boston, Massachusetts"

As delivered:

> "Boston Massachusetts" (no pause)

As written:

> "Campobello, New Brunswick, Canada"

As delivered:

"Campobello New Brunswick Canada" (no pause)

As written:

"Committees are, by nature, timid."

As delivered:

"Committees are by nature, timid." (no pause on first comma)

The most basic principle to remember about phrasing is to think of every action as a separate event, hence, *a declarative sentence* by itself. Don't string separate actions together as one event (or sentence).

7–16

The following sentence should not be read as one event. Instead, treat each action as a declarative event, separated by *pauses*:

"[He walked in the door], [looked around at the people staring at him], [pulling out his .45 caliber pistol], [and began shooting randomly]."

Remember what the purpose of the pause *is*.

Your listeners need time to process what you have to say both logically and—where appropriate—emotionally. They need time to take it in, one item, idea, or event at a time.

Finally, try to observe people telling stories in their own words, giving instructions explaining a concept or a procedure, or just being themselves. If you listen closely, you will be astounded at how much *time* they take in their delivery, how often they *pause*, and how *long* some of those pauses really *are*.

Chapter Eight

REDUNDANCY AND REITERATION

8–1

"This is my friend, Tony. I have known Tony for over twenty years. He's my best friend."

Three very ordinary conversational sentences acquaint Tony with the listener. The first sentence introduces him since he is *new* to the person to whom the sentence is addressed. Here, *Tony* is emphasized. In the second sentence, however, the listener is now conversationally familiar with Tony, so to emphasize his name a second time would be unnecessary and *redundant*. In the third sentence, it would be a similar situation without emphasis on the word *Tony*, but it is now appropriate to use the pronoun *he*, since it would be doubly redundant to use *Tony* one more time.

For a contrasting situation, consider this:

8–2

"XYZ Company is making you this amazing offer. If you buy our gizmo, we'll double the repair period of our warranty. <u>Double</u> it, up to an extra <u>year</u>!"

The first time the word *double* is introduced, it could be emphasized to therefore make the point that the company is making a great offer. This time, however, when *double* is stated again, it is not with *some* emphasis, but with *more* emphasis, as this is hammering home even further the special quality of the offer. This is *reiteration,* or "saying or doing repeatedly." It is *always* emphasized to heighten its dramatic effect. Reiteration occurs often in many medium- and hard-sell commercial spots.

With *redundancy,* when a noun (and rarely another part of speech) has been established, the next time it is stated must be without emphasis. This shows the listener that you are keeping track of what is going on in the script. (People do this naturally when they talk.) If you continue to emphasize what has already been established, it will be very confusing for the listener. When people tell a story or explain a concept, they always naturally keep track of what they have already introduced. Unfortunately, when most untrained people read from copy, they miss what has been established because they are not focused on what they're talking about or on the flow of subject matter. This is typical of the way most people read aloud—from grade school throughout life.

The following are good examples of *redundancy* (redundancies in parenthesis):

8–3

"The <u>White</u> House was constructed in the latter half of the eighteenth <u>century</u> and was completed in the early nineteenth century. At the beginning of the <u>twentieth</u> century, however, when Teddy Roosevelt came to the (White House), he found it in severe disrepair."

Note that *White House* is redundant the second time, as is *century* the second and third times. *Nineteenth* and *twentieth* get the emphasis, not *century*, as does *Roosevelt*, not *White House.*

56

Note that eighteenth, nineteenth, and twentieth are preceding modifiers, but since *century* was established with *eighteenth*, it becomes redundant the second time. Redundancy changes the preceding modifier rule. (See "Parts of Speech: Adjectives.") Here, the modifiers are *emphasized*.

"A long time ago, <u>women</u> finally gained the freedom and right to vote. Now we're fighting a new battle: <u>Illiteracy</u>. One out of four (women) in the United States is functionally illiterate. Nothing holds a (woman) back more than an inability to read and <u>comprehend</u>."

Women gets the emphasis when it is introduced in the first sentence. After that, since it has been established, *women* and *woman* are not highlighted. *Four* gets the emphasis in the second sentence.

Now, here are examples of *reiteration*:

8–4

"You are ordered not to enter at the front gate. I repeat. Do <u>not</u> enter at the front gate." (*Not* is reiterated).

"He had a mental picture, a clear <u>vision</u> of what the future held for him and his family." (Here, *vision* is synonymous with picture, and within the dramatic build in this case, it is a reiteration.)

The following examples offer a variety of situations that involve redundancy, along with special conditions: When a noun is followed by a prepositional phrase, the noun at the end of the phrase gets the emphasis. If the noun at the end is a *redundant* noun, it is not emphasized. The noun in *front* of the prepositional phrase is emphasized. Here are two examples—the first with emphasis on the noun at the end of the prepositional phrase:

8–5

"He had complete mastery over the entire range of the <u>piano</u>."

Now here's the second, with the synonymous word *instrument* as a redundant replacement for *piano*:

> "Having practiced the piano diligently for over twenty years, he attained complete mastery over the entire <u>range</u> of the (instrument)."

Now *range* gets the emphasis, not *instrument*, which is now redundant. (It stands for *piano*.)

Here's an interesting example. This is from a script about a movie director:

> "He was a movie director who was able to take his time with his work and do it in his own way, in an era when <u>most</u> (filmmakers) were <u>deprived</u> of those (luxuries)."

Here, *filmmakers* is redundant because the script has been continually describing his achievements as a *movie director*. *Filmmaker* is synonymous with *movie director* and is therefore redundant. *Luxuries* is redundant as a synonymous word that takes the place of the entire phrase "able to take his time with his work and do it in his own way," both of which are described in another way as *luxuries*.

Look at these examples, where titles are synonymous with names:

8–6

> "The President waited his turn, and <u>Mrs.</u> (Roosevelt) helped with the serving."

Mrs. gets the emphasis since *Roosevelt* is synonymous with the *President*.

> "FDR was one of our most able and effective presidents. (Roosevelt) was born January 30, 1882, in Hyde Park, NY."

Roosevelt replaces FDR and is redundant.

"Ulysses S. <u>Grant</u> was an unpretentious, <u>principled</u> (man)."

Man replaces Ulysses S. Grant.

Redundancy can also apply to an entire phrase, as well as one word.

8–7

"Baggy <u>Pants</u> jumped for joy, as he saw his mother coming back toward their home with a bag of fresh fruit."

Note that *Pants* is functioning as a *surname*.

The follow-up line with the second phrase goes like this:

"Later on, his brother, <u>Droopy</u> (Pants), (saw their mother nearing their home with the fruit.)"

The entire line is not emphasized, because it has been said before, in a slightly different wording. Note also that *Pants* is not emphasized the second time with *Droopy*, as it is also redundant.

Redundancy can apply to a synonymous implication.

8–8

"<u>Jackie Robinson</u> lived through a very difficult era in baseball. The first baseman received many racist taunts from fans and other players, as well as much hate mail."

First baseman is redundant; it stands for Jackie Robinson, who is already established as the subject of the entire script.

Repeating Redundancy

"That man said I must preserve and protect. Protect <u>what</u>? <u>From</u> (what)? For the <u>purpose</u> (of what)?"

Protect is a transitive verb with *what* as its direct object. In the next two short sentences, *what* is not emphasized, because it has become redundant.

Destination on First-Time Introduction

8–9

"The balance between laws and social justice is essential to a free society. Americans must work to improve and <u>maintain</u> (this balance) within their Constitution."

In this interesting example, *balance* is the redundant word in the second sentence. However, when it is introduced in the first sentence, it is not emphasized, because it is followed by a prepositional phrase that further defines it. In other words, a longer *destination*.

Multiple Takes

Be very careful when doing multiple takes.

When doing a new take (or several), approach each take by pretending that on the previous take, the person to whom you were talking has left the room. The person to whom you are talking on the new take is new to your message. Therefore, the message is again a *first-time* message. Paying close attention to this phenomenon will ensure a fresh read each time you do a new take. *You must have consistent repeatability from take to take.*

Many students new to this discipline tend to treat newly introduced words in subsequent takes as redundancies because in their minds, they have introduced the words in an earlier take. This is why it is so necessary to assume that your audience for a new take is someone new. Your message will be fresh.

Keep in mind that if you do ten takes and the tenth is the one they use, it must sound as fresh and new as take *one* was. The relationship between freshly introduced and redundant must be the same, from take to take, throughout the script.

Chapter Nine

DESTINATIONS

Always, when you look over a given phrase, clause, or sentence, ask yourself, "Where am I going with this? Where does it *end*?" This is what defines a *destination*.

Any script line can be extended by a word or words that further *describe* it.

9–1

"It was a most <u>grandiose</u> <u>effort</u>."

"It was a most grandiose, <u>costly</u> <u>effort</u>."

"It was a most grandiose, costly, <u>massive</u> <u>effort</u>."

Note that the last item in each adjective group is also emphasized, because *grandiose*, *costly*, and *massive* make up a *list*. The last word in a list is always emphasized unless it is redundant, or followed by a word or phrase that extends the destination:

9–2

1. "It was the most grandiose, costly, massive effort ever <u>conceived</u>." (further extended by *ever*)
   "It was the most grandiose, costly, massive effort ever conceived (by) <u>man</u>."

Here, *conceived* is not emphasized, because it is extended by the prepositional phrase beginning with *by*.

2. "These are the <u>guidelines</u> you should follow."
   "These are the guidelines you should follow every <u>day</u>."
   (*day* is now the destination)

3. "He is the <u>man</u>."
   "He is the man whom I <u>told</u> you about."
   (pronoun phrase *whom I told you about*, or more correctly, *about whom I <u>told</u> you*, in which case the destination word is a *preposition*)

Note that in most cases, *the last word* of the destination gets the emphasis, especially if it is a *noun*. In the above case, *told* is a *verb*, so it is followed by the pronoun *you*. In the first sentence, *you* and the preposition *about* get no emphasis. The emphasis is still on *told*, however, as it represents the *action*.

Again, ask yourself, "Where is this phrase/clause/sentence going? Where does it end?" In spontaneous conversation, people always do this unconsciously.

Here are several versions of destinations in various lengths for you to practice:

9–3

(Short)
   1. "It was one of the most <u>beautiful</u> of the ancient and sacred <u>sites</u>."

(Extended)
   "It was one of the most <u>beautiful</u> of the ancient and sacred sites (known) to man<u>kind</u>." (Extended by the verb *known*)

(Short)
   2. "In just a few <u>years</u>, he attained a supreme <u>financial</u> status."

62

(Extended)

"In just a few <u>years</u>, he attained a supreme financial status he never <u>dreamed</u> he would <u>attain</u>." (Extended by the implied *that*)

(Short)

   3. "Diligent <u>scholars</u> kept <u>alive</u> the true <u>story</u>."

(Extended)

"Only the labors of a tiny handful of diligent <u>scholars</u> kept alive the true story of the <u>battle</u>." (Extended by the entire phrase *the true story of the battle*)

Note that common single words extend destinations:

who (also *whom*, as in #3 of 9-2 and *whose*, as in #4 of 9-4)
what
when
where
why
that
than
how
as
whether

These are some of the most common words. There are many others.

9–4

Here are several sentences using each of the above words: (parentheses around a word indicates that it is not emphasized)

who

   1. "I saw a <u>news</u> report about a serial murderer."
     "I saw a <u>news</u> report about a serial murderer (who) killed over fifty <u>people</u>."

what

    2. "The <u>committee</u> didn't under<u>stand</u>."

       "The <u>committee</u> didn't understand (what) to <u>do</u> about the problem."

when

    3. "I will let you <u>know</u>."

       "I will let you know (when) I am ready to <u>do</u> this."

whose

    4. "It was only an <u>idea</u>."

       "It was an idea (whose) time had come."

where

    5. "The police had no <u>idea</u>."

       "The <u>police</u> had no idea (where) to <u>look</u> for him."

why

    6. "I <u>know</u> we <u>exist</u>; I just don't know <u>why</u>."

       "I <u>know</u> we <u>exist</u>; I just don't know (why) we're here in the <u>first</u> place."

that

    7. "When the solution to the problem was explained to <u>Henry</u>, he didn't <u>understand</u> it."

       "When the solution to the problem was explained to <u>Henry</u>, he didn't understand (that) he had failed to consider elements (that) might have led to an earlier <u>resolution</u>."

That may also be omitted, but implied:

        "I know (that) you <u>like</u> me."
        "I know you <u>like</u> me."

        "There are many issues (that) we need to <u>discuss</u>."
        "There are many issues we need to <u>discuss</u>."

than

    8. "I was able to carry out my mother's last wishes."

    "I was able to carry out my mother's last wishes farther (than) my sister was able to carry them out."

how

    9. "I hope you will <u>teach</u> me."

    "I hope you will teach me (how) to <u>approach</u> this problem."

as

    10. "Todd did not <u>function</u> well in the <u>military</u>."

    "Todd did not <u>function</u> well (as) a <u>leader</u> in the military."

whether

    11. "He sat down, worrying."

    "He sat <u>down</u>, worrying (whether) or not he had said enough in <u>protest</u>."

Another example of adding one word, *today*, to extend a destination, then changing the ending with other extender words: *again, anymore,* and *here*. This is further discussed in Adverbs in 9-6.

    "It's not supposed to <u>happen</u>."
    "It's not supposed to (happen) <u>today</u>."
    "It's not supposed to (happen) <u>again</u>."
    "It's not supposed to (happen) <u>anymore</u>."
    "It's not supposed to (happen) <u>here</u>."

Note how each of these ending words changes the meaning of the sentence.

Some word combinations can also extend a destination:

more than

    "Our <u>children</u> need us (more than) ever <u>before</u>."

as…as

"This <u>month</u>, we're offering trades (as low as) $4.95 with <u>rebates</u>."

"Jane couldn't believe that her <u>classmate</u> had a wardrobe (as big as) <u>hers</u>."

"If a state's population does not grow (as fast as) <u>others</u>, the situation invites <u>redistricting</u> efforts."

9–5

Destination Words at Ends of Phrases, Clauses and Sentences
These words are emphasized, as they alone are the destinations.

left

    1. There was nothing <u>left</u>.

possible

    2. We can give you the best investing experience <u>possible</u>.

need

    3. We can give you the tools and research you <u>need</u> to realize your long term <u>goals</u>.

        *Note that *you need* is used over and over again on many kinds of scripts, especially business and financial scripts.

expect

    4. Everything you'd <u>expect</u>, and the <u>unexpected</u>.

need

    5. We have everything you <u>need</u> to make your home more <u>beautiful</u>."

want

    6. Our <u>products</u> will give you the look you <u>want</u>.

yet

    7. It's the best effort at a successful exercise regimen <u>yet</u>!

else
> 8. These items are all available at a price that is <u>thousands</u> less than you'll find anywhere <u>else</u>.

put together
> 9. Alan was richer than all of us put <u>together</u>.

else
> 10. He knew Jane better than anyone <u>else</u>.

9–6

Adverbs at Ends of Phrases, Clauses and Sentences

Adverbs that end sentences also act as destinations:

again
> 1. Having created innovation after <u>innovation</u> for the past 50 years, this successful company is making history <u>again</u>, with a brand-new <u>development</u>.

freely
> 2. Buffaloes once roamed <u>freely</u> on their open breeding grounds.

today
> 3. If we nurture our resources <u>today</u>, we'll save more for <u>tomorrow</u>.

well
> 4. If a job is done <u>well</u>, everyone benefits.

Pronouns also extend destinations:

9–7

I

"In spite of what <u>many</u> people think, I did the best (I) could <u>do</u>, under the <u>circumstances</u>."

we

You may also substitute *we* for *I* in the previous sentence.

you

"We'll give you the tools and research (you) <u>need</u> to solve your quality-<u>control</u> problems."

he/she

"The <u>general</u> had won every military campaign (he) <u>led</u>."

it

"<u>Many</u> people do not have a historical understanding of how the United <u>States</u> became the modern nation (it) is <u>today</u>."

one

"The more self-reliant (one) <u>is</u>, the more <u>secure</u> one will <u>feel</u>."

Infinitives also extend destinations:

Infinitives are expressed by action and state of a verb that is not limited by connection with a subject.

For our purposes, the infinitive is almost always preceded by *to*. In keeping with the concept of destinations, it is important to understand that infinitives *always* extend a destination.

Some examples:
(Remember, parenthesis means no emphasis on that word)

9–8

"I am here (to) <u>help</u> you."

"He didn't want (to) <u>trouble</u> the poor woman."

"They made an attempt (to) <u>stop</u> the <u>rioting</u>."

"There is nothing (to) <u>equal</u> it in splendor and <u>beauty</u>."

"This country came (to) be <u>recognized</u> by its approach to <u>manufacturing</u>."

"He had the audacity (to) thumb his <u>nose</u> at the world."

"They were going (to) build the tallest skyscraper in the <u>world</u>."

"As soon as it was safe for him (to) <u>travel</u>, they took him to <u>Europe</u>."

Note that in every example above, the infinitive is preceded by a sentence that can stand on its own as a complete sentence, but when the infinitive phrase is added, it creates a longer sentence with an extended meaning.

Destinations are also extended by *prepositional phrases*:

Note also that infinitives can be *transitive* or *intransitive*.

Remember that *prepositions* denote position or direction, and prepositional phrases can also be *settings*; i.e., time or place. For all practical purposes in voice over, prepositions should almost never be emphasized.

One notable exception is illustrated below:

9–9

"America is a country <u>of</u> the people, <u>by</u> the people, and <u>for</u> the people."

The prepositions are emphasized in this example because we are *comparing* prepositions.

Here is a list of many common prepositions, each followed by a sentence using each preposition in parenthesis:

about
"I knew they were talking (about) my <u>girlfriend</u>."

above
"The men were working in the attic (above) my <u>office</u>."

across
"Be <u>careful</u> before you walk (across) the <u>street</u>."

against
"The committee was (against) keeping its chairman."

around
"Prosperity is just (around) the corner."

behind
"Sally looked (behind) the door for her lost pendant."

beneath
"The divers found the gold bars (beneath) a thick layer of sand and mud."

beside
"He leadeth me (beside) the still waters."

between
"Even though the disagreement had the potential for involving others, it was kept (between) the two originators."

by
"I want this job finished (by) the end of day tomorrow."

by way of
"You can get to Boston (by way of) Hartford."

down
"Suzy loved to ride (down) the water slide."

except
"Everyone came to the party (except) Fred."

from
"He received a dear John letter (from) his angry fiancée."

in front of
"Henry didn't want to look bad (in front of) his friends."

in place of
"Jimmy was selected (in place of) the man whom many thought was more qualified."

into

"With such a hostile <u>attitude</u>, you could get (into) a lot of <u>trouble</u>."

like

"Molly is beginning to look a lot (like) her <u>sister</u>."

near

"Be <u>patient</u>; we're getting (near) the <u>end</u> of the presentation."

of

"Several (of) the <u>survivors</u> were in critical <u>condition</u>."

off

"Please get (off) the <u>couch</u>."

on

"The workers (on) the <u>waterfront</u> planned a strike to address a number of grievances."

onto

"To <u>save</u> himself, Tom climbed (onto) a large wooden <u>door</u> floating in the <u>water</u>."

out of

"With nightfall approaching, the injured men knew they were running (out of) time."

past

"He was afraid to look (past) his immediate <u>prospects</u>."

since

"She hasn't seen her <u>son</u> (since) last January."

through

"After fifty years of <u>marriage</u>, a husband and <u>wife</u> know they have been (through) a <u>lot</u> together."

to

"Philip went (to) <u>UCLA</u> to apply for a <u>scholarship</u>."

toward

"Mary's anger (toward) <u>Mark</u> <u>continued</u> for over a <u>week</u>."

under

"He found the frightened <u>dog</u> hiding (under) a <u>bush</u>."

underneath

"The police found a <u>bomb</u> hidden (underneath) the spare <u>tire</u> in the suspect's <u>SUV</u>."

until/by

"Wait (until) the first <u>shot</u> is fired (by) the <u>enemy</u> before you <u>fire</u>."

upon

"Once (upon) a <u>time</u>, there were three little <u>pigs</u>."

To give you a sense of comparison between the short length before the preposition and the longer length with it added, here are several other examples. Note how the *points of emphasis* change, according to the dramatic requirements:

9-10

to

    1. "They bore him <u>away</u>."

       "They bore him away (to) the lake in <u>Maine</u>."

about

    2. "The farmer constantly <u>worried</u>."

       "The farmer worried (about) getting his <u>crops</u> harvested on <u>time</u>."

in

    3. "Unlike most of his <u>friends,</u> he knew he was <u>special</u>."

       "Unlike most of his friends (in) <u>school</u>, he knew he was <u>special</u>."

of

    4. "From the suburban <u>town</u>, they took the <u>train</u>."
        "From the suburban town (of) <u>Elmira</u>, they took the train (to) New York <u>City</u>."

since

    5. "He enjoyed working with <u>horses</u>, which he had always <u>loved</u>."
        "He enjoyed working with horses, which he had loved (since) <u>boyhood</u>."

Prepositional Phrases *only* with Extended Destinations:

9-11

of

    1. "The rise (of) modern <u>Germany</u>."

of

    2. "The birth (of) modern <u>jazz</u>."

of

    3. "The growth (of) <u>populism</u>."

of

    4. "The theory (of) <u>relativity</u>."

of

    5. "The party (of) the first <u>part</u>."

in

    6. "The youngest president (in) <u>history</u>."

as

    7. "Described him (as) our only true <u>leader</u>."

on

    8. "Identified (on) a <u>personal</u> level."

with

    9. "Working (with) the <u>air</u> conditioner turned up <u>full</u>."

like

    10. "Looked (like) a man who had won the <u>lottery</u>."

Other considerations about prepositions:

There are many situations where the presence of a preposition will not necessarily mean that the word that precedes it will be deemphasized. There may be dramatic considerations to observe:

9-12

like

    1. "He styled his hair in a stubble, slicked <u>back</u>, (like) an old man's <u>crewcut</u>."

to

    2. "You need to pay more <u>attention</u> (to) what you are <u>doing</u>."

of

    3. "There were massive <u>killings</u> (of) migratory <u>birds</u>."

with

    4. "They expect a firm <u>price</u>, (with) quality <u>work</u>."

at

    5. "He yelled (at) the <u>audience</u>."

for

    6. "It is against the <u>law</u> (for) people to own automatic <u>weapons</u>."

from

    7. "They were <u>prevented</u> (from) voting their <u>choices</u>."

by

8. "America came to be large identified (by) its <u>movies</u>."

with

9. "Solomon is <u>synonymous</u> (with) judicial <u>wisdom</u>."

against

10. "Jefferson swore eternal <u>hostility</u> (against) every form of <u>tyranny</u>."

after

11. "The economy of the United <u>States</u> got a jump <u>start</u> (after) World War <u>II</u>."

along

12. "Although he enjoyed the <u>trip</u>, he seemed to <u>tire</u> (along) the <u>way</u>."

among

13. "She felt <u>comfortable</u> (among) her close <u>friends</u>."

before

14. "Her mother wanted to visit her <u>sister</u> one more <u>time</u> (before) she <u>died</u>."

below

15. "There was grave <u>danger</u> (below) the deck of the <u>ship</u>."

according to

16. "The economy may <u>falter</u> next year (according to) recent <u>reports</u>."

because of

17. "I made many <u>mistakes</u> (because of) my failure to <u>look</u> before I <u>leaped</u>."

during

    18. "The congregation kept very <u>quiet</u> during the <u>funeral</u> service."

in

    19. "I want this mess cleaned <u>up</u> (in) ten <u>minutes</u>."

in spite of

    20. "We have decided to accept you as a <u>member,</u> (in spite of) your unfriendly <u>manner</u>."

on account of

    21. "He had to stop <u>running,</u> (on account of) his <u>pain</u>."

over

    22. "The planes made <u>pass</u> after pass (over) the mesmerized <u>onlookers</u>."

up

    23. "My dog chased a <u>squirrel</u> (up) a <u>tree</u>."

with

    24. "I'm surprised that Emily didn't' become <u>famous</u> (with) all of her <u>talent</u>."

within

    25. "Over two hundred animal and <u>plant</u> species became <u>extinct,</u> (within) the life span of <u>most</u> of us."

This is easily one of the most important chapters in this book. In my experience, nothing confounds voice over talent more than the concept of destinations.

Watch carefully for words and phrases that extend destinations. They are very easy to miss.

Chapter Ten

COMPARING AND CONTRASTING

Comparison and *contrast* describe the relationship two entities have with each other. By *relationship*, I mean how they agree or disagree with each other and how they are similar or different. When these entities are compared or contrasted, the *second* entity—the one *doing* the comparing or contrasting—gets the emphasis.

The following are examples of comparisons and contrasts as they apply to nouns, adjectives, adverbs, pronouns, prepositions, conjunctions, and yes, *prefixes*.

Listen to the audio tracks for the points of emphasis.

Nouns (the people, the places, the things)

10–1

"I prefer <u>Paris</u> to <u>London</u>." (*Paris* vs. *London*)

"A <u>house</u> is not a <u>home</u>." (*house* vs. *home*)

"It's safer to be <u>flying</u> than <u>driving</u>." (*flying* vs. *driving*)

"This is a <u>loan</u>, not a <u>gift</u>." (*loan* vs. *gift*)

"Tim wanted Nora to be his <u>wife</u>, not his <u>girlfriend</u>." (*wife* vs. *girlfriend*)

"His career was full of great <u>successes</u>, but there were many <u>failures</u> along the way." (*successes* vs. *failures*)

Verbs (the action)

10–2

"Instead of <u>talking</u> to the group calmly, he was <u>shouting</u> his message." (*talking* vs. *shouting*)

"Empires will <u>rise</u>, and empires will <u>fall</u>." (*rise* vs. *fall*)

"After it <u>floated</u> for a few minutes, the badly damaged canoe <u>sank</u>." (*floated* vs. *sank*)

"He lived and <u>died</u> by the sword." (*lived* vs. *died*)

This also follows the rule applying to two entities separated by a conjunction, so there is no emphasis on *lived*.

Adjectives (modify nouns)

10–3

"Norma was very <u>beautiful</u> but, unfortunately, not very <u>smart</u>." Adjectives *beautiful* and *smart* modify the noun *Norma*. (*beautiful* vs. s*mart*)

"Do you want a <u>red</u> pepper or a <u>green</u> pepper?"

Adjectives *red* and *green* modify the noun *pepper*. (*red* vs. *green*)

*Note that in the first two examples, the pauses in the reading on the audio examples are inconsistent with the punctuation in the written versions, as they sound more natural as delivered. You will see this phenomenon at work in other examples in this book. Written punctuation is not always a reliable indicator of where to pause.

"Maria did not sound as pleasing on her <u>low</u> notes as she did on her <u>high</u> notes."

Adjectives *low* and *high* modify the noun *notes*. (*low* vs. *high*)

78

"We no longer manufacture women's shoes, only men's shoes." Adjectives *women's* and *men's* modify the noun *shoes*. (*women's* vs. *men's*)

"Mike was pleased about the outcome; Terry was disappointed." Adjective *pleased* modifies the noun *Mike*; *disappointed* modifies *Terry*. *Mike* and *Terry* also compare. (*pleased* vs. *disappointed*, *Mike* vs. *Terry*)

"The festival was expected to draw a large attendance, but it turned out to be very meager."

Adjectives *large* and *meager* modify the noun *attendance*. (*large* vs. *meager*)

Large is not emphasized, as it is a *preceding modifier*.

"Some Wall Street CEOs make over a hundred million dollars, while the average guy is lucky to make over a hundred thousand."

Adjectives *million* and *thousand* modify the noun *dollars*.

(*million* vs. *thousand*, *CEOs* vs. *average guy*)

Again, million is not emphasized, as in the previous example.

"Tom may be a good piano player, but John is the best." Adjectives *good* and *best* modify the noun *piano player* as previously.

(*Tom* vs. *John*, *good* vs. *best*)

Adverbs (modify verbs, adjectives, and other adverbs)

10–4

"Sally did very well in school, but Amy did very poorly." Adverbs *well* and *poorly* modify verb *did*. (*Sally* vs. *Amy*, *well* vs. *poorly*)

"The work went on quite rapidly, but within a few hours, less rapidly."

Adverbs *quite* and *less* modify the adverb *rapidly*. (*quite* vs. *less*)

79

Note that rapidly is emphasized the first time, but the second time it is *redundant*.

"The wealthy woman was elegantly beautiful; her maid, though attractive herself, was <u>commonly</u> beautiful."

Adverbs *elegantly* and *commonly* modify the adjective *beautiful*. Note emphasis changes as before.

(*elegantly* vs. *commonly*)

"Is this a wholly owned subsidiary or <u>partially</u> owned?" Adverbs *wholly* and *partially* modify the adjective *owned*. (*wholly* vs. *partially*)

"Rather than break the news to her gently, he did it <u>bluntly</u>." Adverbs *gently* and *bluntly* modify the verb *did*.

(*gently* vs. *bluntly*)

Pronouns

10–5

"Do you want to go with him, or with <u>me</u>?" (*him* vs. *me*)

Possessive Pronouns

"Is this your money or <u>his</u> money?" (*your* vs. *his*)

"It all comes down to whether the police believe my story or <u>his</u> story." (*my* vs. *his*)

"Not my will, but <u>thine</u> be done." (*my* vs. *thine*)

Prepositions

10–6

"Are you for me or <u>against</u> me?" (*for* vs. *against*)

"Do you want the flowers placed on the table or <u>beside</u> it?" (*on* vs. *beside*)

"Rather than go <u>around</u> the tunnel, the group made the decision to go <u>through</u> it." (*around* vs. *through*)

"Do they want in or <u>out</u> of the deal?" (*in* vs. *out*)

Prefixes

10–7

"Are you married or <u>un</u>married?"

"Is this the inbound train or the <u>out</u>bound train?"

"They are trained to train the <u>un</u>trained."

"Will this project be built from scratch or <u>re</u>built?"

"The buttoned-down professor <u>un</u>buttoned a little."

"The Bolsheviks barred <u>non</u>-Bolsheviks from membership."

All the rules of weight on words change when we compare and contrast virtually any part of speech. The following are several examples for practice.

Double (or More) Comparisons and Contrasts

10–8

Often, a contrast may exist between more than two entities:

"The <u>cat</u> <u>hissed</u>, and the <u>dog</u> <u>growled</u>."

"He had <u>cereal</u> for <u>breakfast</u>, a <u>sandwich</u> for <u>lunch</u>, and a <u>steak</u> for <u>dinner</u>."

"If you are <u>for</u> <u>him</u>, you are <u>against</u> <u>me</u>."

"<u>Today's</u> <u>anchors</u> were <u>yesterday's</u> <u>correspondents</u>."

"The article would be written about <u>football's</u> <u>best</u> <u>player</u> or <u>baseball's</u> <u>worst</u> <u>manager</u>."

Implied Comparisons or Contrasts

In consideration of what subject matter has been introduced, a contrast may be implied. The voice over artist must be very aware of all details in the script, to be able to apply this concept wherever it fits the situation:

10–9

> "The project helped residents fix up their houses and improve the neighborhood, but it was not enough for the neighborhood's <u>needier</u> homeowners, who were not able to fix up their houses on their own."

Here, *needier* is given weight because *homeowners* is another word for residents. The introduction of the adjective *needier* into the situation implies that the other residents previously stated are getting along without additional help.

Don't anticipate a comparison or contrast unless it is immediately fulfilled.

10–10

> (Immediate) "I have a <u>black</u> cat; my friend Suzy has a <u>white</u> cat."

> (Delayed) "I have a black cat. He is a huge cat with a fluffy tail. My friend Suzy has a <u>white</u> cat with a <u>bobtail</u>."

The previous examples are designed to give you many clues where to look for comparisons and contrasts. The following examples are practice exercises. Listen to them carefully on the audio.

Pronouns

10–11

> "If <u>you</u> can do it, <u>I</u> can." (comparison)

> "Maybe <u>you</u> know what happened here, but <u>I</u> don't." (contrast)

Nouns

10–12

"Is that a <u>zebra</u> or a <u>horse</u>?" (comparison)

"That's not a <u>house</u>; it's a <u>palace</u>!" (contrast)

Intransitive Verbs

10–13

"I would rather <u>walk</u> than <u>run</u>." (comparison)

"She didn't know whether to <u>giggle</u> or to <u>laugh</u>!" (comparison)

"<u>Living</u> beats <u>dying</u>." (contrast)

"You can <u>cry</u> if you want to, but the story makes me <u>smile</u>." (contrast)

Adjectives

10–14

"Your painting is <u>good</u>; hers is <u>better</u>." (comparison)

"Your painting is <u>good</u>; hers is <u>awful</u>!" (contrast)

Adverbs

10–15

"I sent the package early to make sure it arrives <u>where</u> it's supposed to and <u>when</u> it's supposed to." (comparison)

"I wanted it to arrive <u>soon</u>; it arrived <u>late</u>." (contrast)

Prepositions

10–16

"Are you <u>in</u> my circle or <u>out</u> of it?"

"We may have to do this deal <u>under</u> the table instead of <u>on</u> it."

"America is a government <u>of</u> the people."

(straight ahead—no comparison or contrast)

"America is a government <u>of</u> the people, <u>by</u> the people, and <u>for</u> the people." (comparison)

"America is <u>for</u> the people, not <u>against</u> them." (contrast)

(Outside/Inside) "Outside the house, the weather had turned bitter cold, but <u>in</u>side the house, it was warm and cozy."

(Outside/Inside)n "Some of the children played in the backyard in the bitter cold, but <u>inside</u>, the other children relaxed in the warmth and coziness of the house."

Outside is <u>implied</u>. Therefore, to contrast with it, we emphasize the prefix *in*.

Double Comparisons

<u>10–17</u>

"Today's <u>anchors</u> were <u>yesterday's</u> <u>correspondents</u>." (*Today's* is not emphasized, as we don't know the comparison is coming until you say *yesterday's*.)

"I seem only to see black <u>dogs</u> by <u>day</u> and white <u>cats</u> by <u>night</u>." (*dogs* vs. *cats* and *black* vs. *white*)

Be on the alert for any situation that even *suggests* a comparison or contrast, as you must be prepared to intensify the points where the comparisons and contrasts occur.

Chapter Eleven
DIALOGUE AND QUOTATIONS

Dialogue

In most commercial and narration situations, *dialogue* is seldom used. However, there is one area where the ability to handle dialogue is vital: *audiobooks*—specifically, children's and adult fiction audiobooks, for the most part.

Dialogue situations fall into three component parts: the *quote* (what is spoken), *who says it* (he/she/they said/asked/replied, etc.), and the *description of the action* by you, the narrator.

The *quote* is the most animated because it is spontaneous speech or conversation in the moment. *Who says it* (he said/she said) is a complete throwaway, with no animation whatsoever, and it immediately follows the quote with a short pause. In the *description of the action*, you assume and keep the role of the person telling the story.

In many books, there may be pages and pages of dialogue where these three elements interact with one another. As the dialogue moves from one person to another, change the pitch, timbre, and animation *only in the quotes*.

There is no change at all in *who says it*. However, there may be mild changes in the description of the action, if there are some dramatic shifts in the telling of the story.

Listen carefully on the audio tracks to the following examples:

11–1

1. He walked over to the package and picked it up. "I wouldn't open it, if I were you," she said. "I'll open it if I want to," he quipped, glaring at her menacingly. The package exploded in his face and threw him backward. "Oh my God," she said. "They've killed him."

2. His mother was pleased. He had brought home a perfect report card for the first time. "I'm so proud of you," she gushed. "I know this will be one of many positives in your life." His father's reaction, however, was as usual. "Why couldn't you do this two years ago?" he quipped, "Because you're very inconsistent, and probably always will be." Jimmy knew not to reply, as it would be a fruitless effort.

3. Maria was looking forward to her wedding that afternoon to Jack. She smiled at her sister, who was helping her with her wedding wardrobe. "I know Jack and I are going to be very happy," she sighed. "Are you sure you're over Paul?" Olivia asked. "I don't care if I ever see him again," Maria replied. "You're seeing him right now," said a man's voice coming in from the adjacent room. "Oh my god, it's Paul!" Maria said. "Paul, I think it would be better for everyone if you left right now," Olivia said. "Not until we've talked this out," he replied. "I don't want her to make a mistake that will ruin both our lives."

In these stories, there are two, then three characters. It is up to you to adjust your voice to convince the listener that there are distinctly different people talking. We're not doing character voices here, but you need only to suggest, mostly by pitch change, the distinction between female and male subjects as well as between people of the same sex.

The following children's story will be much more interesting to the listener if the quotes are done in character voices:

11–2

Once upon a time, in the walls between the studs of the rehearsal rooms in the basement of the Grand Ole Opry, there lived four rural redneck rats, who had the best rodent country band in all the cellars of Nashville. Billy Bob played the bass guitar, Bodeen the acoustic and electric, Buck the fiddle, and Bubba did the vocals and pedal steel on the side.

They had two big hits—"Big Cheese in a Country Band," written by Billy Bob and Bubba, and "I've Fallen in a Rat Trap Over You," written by Bodeen and Buck.

One day, while they was working on new material, Billy Bob piped up and asked, "Why don't we do somethin' different this time, like a 'he done her wrong' song?"

"How about a song about a fairy tale character?" asked Bodeen.

"Them ideas is goin' nowhere," said Buck. "We need somethin' about a real macho man."

Bubba's eyes lit up. "I got it! Not one he-man, but a whole bunch! 'Beer Night at the Drunken Rat Bar.'"

Sure enough, "Beer Night at the Drunken Rat Bar" became their third and biggest hit, and they never had to pay for another beer anywhere again.

To review, *dialogue* consists of three entities:

1. *The quote itself* (what is spoken)

2. *Who says it* (he said, she said)

3. *The description of the action* (the narrator, telling the story)

As you practice moving through these three elements, make them as different from one another as possible. Listen to audiobook performances by top talents as models for your own delivery.

Quotations

If there is one key concept to remember about quotations, it is this: the quote itself is *out of context* with the story you are telling. It has its *own* context because what is said in the quote applies to the context of the quote itself, *in the mind-set at the time when the person being quoted said it*. When we quote a source, we are going back in time to the moment he or she said it.

Here's an example:

11–3

Of the Irish Rebellion of 1916, the British writer Cyril Connelly wrote, "There is nothing to equal it as a drama, except the first months of the Spanish Civil War."

Note that the reference to Connelly is in the past tense (*said*), while Connelly's reference to nothing equaling the rebellion as a drama is in the present tense because it was his take on the situation at the time he made the quoted statement.

The quote is always a reference to the past, while the quote itself is in a *here and now* moment to the person saying it.

In another consideration, what may have been repeated several times in the main body of the story is now said as new and fresh in the quote.

Why? Because the person to whom the quote is attributed is talking about a subject that is fresh to him or her. In a script about church and state, in which *religion* is talked about over and over, there follows a quote by Thomas Jefferson:

11–4

"The battle over church and state is as old as religion itself. Religious leaders tell their congregations whom to vote for. When asked about the influence of religion on politics, they deny its influence. When asked his own opinion, Thomas Jefferson said, "Religion is a subject on which I am most scrupulously reserved. It is a matter between every man and his maker.""

Keep in mind also that when you quote anyone, male or female, you should use a slight change in pitch and timbre in your voice to indicate the introduction of a person other than you. It does not have to be done in character (as would be the case in a children's story or an animated piece).

Chapter Twelve

COLLOQUIAL RECOGNITION

One of the least observed characteristics that contribute heavily to a natural sounding delivery is the *colloquial* phrase. By definition, *colloquial* means "characteristic of informal speech and writing." Colloquial sentences defy the basic rules of starting easy, building, and ending strong. Sentences containing colloquial phrases work in the opposite way: they begin strong and end by quickly trailing off. Consider the following sentences, which are marked for emphasis according to a *straight*, or literal, pattern of delivery. Following each example is the same sentence marked for a colloquial delivery. You can hear them both on the accompanying audio tracks. Listen to how much more natural and conversational the colloquial reads are:

12–1

(straight)	The boss wants to see <u>you</u>.
(colloquial)	The <u>boss</u> (wants to see you).
(straight)	My wife (husband) works too <u>hard</u>.
(colloquial)	My wife (husband) <u>works</u> (too hard).
(straight)	Our survival is at <u>stake</u>.
(colloquial)	Our <u>survival</u> (is at stake).

(straight)   I don't want to be with you <u>anymore</u>.

(colloquial)   I don't want to <u>be</u> (with you anymore).

Two in a row:

(straight)   There's automatic overdraft protection <u>available</u>, so your checks don't <u>bounce</u>.

(colloquial)   There's automatic <u>overdraft</u> protection (available), so your <u>checks</u> (don't bounce).

Colloquial endings are *passive*; that is, they are distinguished by throwaway endings that trail off. Listen to how contrived the straight reads sound compared to the colloquial reads, which come across in the same way people use these expressions every day. Learn to identify them.

Chapter Thirteen
ACTIVE AND PASSIVE VOICE

Closely allied with colloquial expressions are sentences that end with a *passive voice* treatment. Passive voice means just as it sounds: sentences that end not with a bang but with a whimper. Passive voice is sometimes used only to add *variety* in the writing (for example, this sentence). It can also add a sense of informality to the script, as well as enliven the drama. In the majority of sentences in English, the <u>subject</u> does the action stated by the verb.

<u>13–1</u>

"The contestant ate at least twenty-five hot dogs."

The *contestant* (subject) does the *eating* (verb).

"Anne rode her bicycle to work."

Anne (subject) is doing the *riding* (verb).

Since the subject does the acting via the verb, sentences such as these are in the *active voice*.

As long as the sentence has a direct object (a noun acted on by the verb), we can change the normal order of most active-voice sentences, by making a *subject* out of the original *object* so that it is being acted upon by the v*erb*. This is *passive voice*. Here are the original sentences, "passive-ized":

13–2

"At least twenty-five hot dogs (subject) were eaten (verb) by the contestant."

"Her bicycle (subject) was ridden (verb) by Anne to work."

Most books on writing recommend sticking to active voice. With passive voice, the reader has to work a bit harder since the sentence construction alters the normal *doer-action* (receiver of action) flow.

Here are more examples:

13–3

Active Voice

"At each event, the speaker (subject/doer) reads (verb/action) one passage (object/receiver of action) from a classic novel."

Passive Voice

"At each event, one passage (receiver of action/subject) from a classic novel was read (verb/action) by a speaker (doer of action)."

Active Voice

"Repair crews (doer-subject) will bring in (verb/action) planeloads (subject/receiver) of aircraft parts to fix the damage caused by the hurricane."

Passive Voice

"Planeloads of aircraft parts (receiver of action/subject) will be brought (verb/action) in by repair crews (doer of action) to fix the damages caused by the hurricane."

Active Voice

"We will gain some unique benefits from this experience."

Passive Voice

"There are some unique benefits to be gained from this experience."

Remember that most of the time, for the sake of simplicity and direct action, *active voice* is preferable. Passive voice may be preferred, however, when the doer of the action is not known, wanted, or needed.

13–4

"The *votes* have been tallied; the *returns* have been analyzed."

"Occasionally, the *meaning* of it all is missed."

Passive voice may also be preferred if the *action* of the sentence is emphasized, rather than the *doer* of the action. In this case, the *end* of the passive statement is emphasized.

13–5

"The election process was almost undone by right-wing extremists."

"The young dancer was pushed for hours by her overzealous mentor."

Here again are several examples, with the straight reading first, then the passive (correct *reading* version):

13–6

Incorrectly read as: "A musical was written to commemorate the historical event."

Correctly read as: "A musical (was written) to commemorate the historical event."

Incorrectly read as: "New analytical tools are being developed every day."

Correctly read as: "New analytical tools (are being developed) every day."

Incorrectly read as: "A new canal will be built to stem the destructive waters."

Correctly read as: "A new canal (will be built) to stem the destructive waters."

Incorrectly read as: "Many chunks of rock were <u>removed</u> from the new <u>beach</u> sand."

Correctly read as: "Many chunks of <u>rock</u> (were removed) from the new <u>beach</u> sand."

Once again, listen to the audio. Do you hear the difference? Which do you think sounds more natural, more real?

Here are three practice exercises. Identify the places where passive voice occurs:

13–7

"The western saw justice done."

"Orders were given to suppress the truth about the massacre."

"As we enjoy each other's company, doors will slam, and dogs will bark, and someone will play the piano."

Here is an *infinitive*, used in a passive setting:

13–8

"There are some unique <u>benefits</u> (to be gained) from this experience."

Many professionals, especially in radio and TV announcer positions, give me the impression that they do not understand the passive voice concept, and as a consequence, their interpretations inevitably sound contrived and unnatural. Take time to learn and absorb this concept.

Chapter Fourteen
Lists and Patterns

Lists can be deceptive and complicated. There are basically two approaches to interpreting lists. When you encounter a list, ask yourself this: Do I need to focus on each item in the list as a separate image or event to be experienced individually, or are the listed entities *connected* as a related group?

Here are two examples of focusing on *each element* of the list. Separate each one as a statement with a declarative ending, as if there were a period after each. Pause between each *adjective* in the following example:

14–1

1. "Many found the king to be wise, <u>accomplished</u>, <u>broadminded</u>, <u>calm</u>, and <u>sensible</u>. Others found him <u>treacherous</u>, <u>mean-spirited</u>, <u>manipulative</u>, and <u>deceptive</u>."

Each of these listed adjectives contains, on the one hand, positive and reassuring emotional responses to a trusted monarch, and on the other, negative and troubling responses to a man they fear and mistrust.

2. "Andy was a lovable man. A considerate <u>father</u>. A loving <u>husband</u>. A God-fearing <u>follower</u>. A man who led by his own <u>example</u>."

Now the items in the list are *nouns*. This list is punctuated by *periods*, not commas, although the writer could have used commas. The periods are more suggestive of the speaker's one-at-a-time insightful observations of Andy's character, and a slightly longer pause between each is recommended for maximum dramatic effect.

Here are two examples of a *connected* list:

14–2

1. "It enlisted men, nations, and <u>money</u> on an unimaginable scale." (Read as a connected group without pauses.)

2. "It helped to shatter the myths, values, and <u>traditions</u> of America itself." (Read as a connected group, with short *pauses* because these are qualities, each of which supports the concept of being American. The pauses, in this case, give more *dramatic impact* to these qualities.)

Many lists, particularly those in which each element is delivered as a statement, offer pausing and even breathing opportunities, especially between the penultimate list element and the last list element, which may or may not be separated by a conjunction. Remember that the *pause* is a powerful dramatic tool.

In virtually all lists, the conjunction leading into the last item in the list will be an *and* or an *or*. (See **Conjunctions** in "Grama-Drama.")

Here are some examples with the conjunctions:

14–3

"The view from the <u>mountaintop</u> was <u>spectacular</u>, (pause) at once <u>serene</u>, (longer pause) and almost <u>holy</u>."

"He loved the way she <u>walk</u>ed (pause), her warm <u>smile</u>, (longer pause) and the bright <u>sparkle</u> in her eyes."

"I love <u>apples</u>, (pause) <u>oranges</u>, (pause) <u>grapes</u>, (pause) <u>pineapples</u>, (longer pause) and <u>bananas</u>."

Note that the *last* item in the list gets the strongest *emotional* emphasis (not *volume*).

"Listen. The sound of <u>china</u> and <u>crystal</u>."

"He was pleased and <u>proud</u> at the singular honor."

In the first sentence, the nouns *china* and *crystal* are *both* emphasized for dramatic effect. In the second sentence, the adjectives *pleased* and *proud* are also emphasized for the same purpose.

Here are some examples *without* conjunctions:

14–4

"He was shy, (pause) with<u>drawn</u>, (pause) <u>lackluster</u>, (longer pause) <u>dispassionate</u>."

"A man without <u>conscience</u>. (pause) <u>hypocritical</u>, (pause) <u>mean-spirited</u>, (pause) <u>philistine</u>, (longer pause) <u>cruel</u>."

Again, very strong emphasis on the last descriptive word in the list, as these are both very dramatic sentences.

Patterns

Look for *patterns*, especially in *lists*.

14–5

"<u>Today</u>. <u>Tomorrow</u>. And in the <u>future</u>."

Future gets the heaviest hit of the three, as it is the *last* in the list.

"You have it <u>all</u>—a self-assured <u>manner</u>, a distinctive <u>air</u>, a <u>personality</u> that <u>defines</u> you."

Personality gets the big hit, following the buildup in *patterns*.

"Most alcoholics hate <u>drinking</u>, hate the <u>taste</u>, hate <u>themselves</u>."

Themselves is a *pronoun*, but in context, it is used as a *direct object*. Normally, if we only said, "Alcoholics hate (themselves)," it would be as a no-emphasis reflexive pronoun. However, in this context, it is at the end of a patterned, building *list*, with the hit on *themselves* to finalize the buildup.

Be aware that lists are not always punctuated by *commas*, as in the first example above.

Go over this chapter carefully, as it is important for you to understand how to make lists dramatically interesting to your listener instead of boringly droning through them.

Chapter Fifteen
HOW TO INFLECT QUESTIONS

Many of the questions expressed in scripts you will deliver are *rhetorical*; that is, they are read as *statements*, with no answer being expected.

Listen carefully to the recorded readings of the following examples, as they will give you a strong sense of how to inflect them. Once again, the points of emphasis are underlined:

15–1

Rhetorical

"I guess there aren't any <u>answers</u> to this problem, <u>are</u> there?"

"Well, what do you know about <u>that</u>?"

"Isn't that a gorgeous <u>sunset</u>?"

"What's <u>wrong</u> with you?"

"Well, aren't you the <u>smart</u> one?"

"Isn't it <u>grand</u>, living in <u>Paris</u>?"

15–2

Insistent and *emphatic* are questions that expect answers:

"Where <u>are</u> you?"

"What are we going to do about the rising <u>crime</u> in our <u>neighborhood</u>?"

"How much does it <u>cost</u>?"

"What's the <u>answer</u>?"

"How will you <u>cope</u>?"

"What will you <u>do</u>?"

"Where will you <u>go</u>?"

"Where's my <u>stuff</u>?"

"Do we need to get <u>tough</u> or show some <u>leniency</u>?"

"Where's the <u>sports</u> page?"

Others are *true questions* and end with *upward* inflections. Upward inflections are rare.

15–3

"Is that <u>you</u> I hear?"

"Are you <u>listening</u> to me?"

"What's <u>wrong</u>?"

"Is this the road to Pismo <u>Beach</u>?"

"Were you <u>aware</u> of this?"

"Am I <u>disturbing</u> you?"

"Will I <u>live</u> through this?"

"Did Tom like the <u>movie</u>?"

"Is <u>that</u> all there is?"

"Am I going to have <u>trouble</u> with you?"

Still others may be combinations of upward and downward inflections:

"Are you my <u>friend</u> (upward) or <u>not</u>?" (downward)

"Is this <u>yours</u> (upward) or <u>his</u>?" (downward)

101

Chapter Sixteen

DIPHTHONGS

One dictionary defines *diphthong* as "two vowel sounds joined in one syllable to form one speech sound (as with *ou* in *out*)." Another describes it as "a sound made by gliding from one vowel into another (as with *ea* in *create*)." *Both* definitions are valid.

Diphthongs and Regional Dialects

Adding Diphthongs:

A significant number of people have difficulty with diphthongs. In the case of the words *out* or *about*, many southerners, in particular, pronounce *ou* not as "*ow*" but "*aaow*." This means two perceptibly distinct vowels instead of one.

Omitting Diphthongs:

Conversely, the opposite is true with the pronunciation of *ea* in *create*. I have heard this pronounced on a television ad as "*crated*," when it should have been pronounced as "*creeayted*," with a very distinct pronunciation of *e* and *a* within the smooth transition from one to the other.

Within words, there are many combinations of vowels that are pronounced as one syllable, while others require gliding one vowel into another, some with a barely perceptible change and others with a very *distinct* change. Here is a list of those words, divided into two columns. Study them carefully, and as suggested in other chapters, continue to review these words until they have become part of your linguistic arsenal:

16–1

Sounding as one syllable:

Sounding as two syllables, but barely perceptible in the flow from one vowel to another:

bread	meadow	about	joy
breath	measure	bare	loud
dead	pain	boy	mountain
deaf	peasant	broil	oil
death	pleasant	brown	ouch
drain	pleasure	care	out
dread	read	chair	pear
feather	spread	coin	point
goal	stain	couch	poison
goat	stead	count	power
head	sweat	cow	proud
instead	sweater	dare	share
jealousy	thread	dowel	shout
jeopardy	threat	down	shower
juice	tread	fair	soil
lead	treasure	fire	stair
leather	weather	frail	thousand
		growl	tower
		hair	voice
		hour	vowel
		jail	wear
		join	wire

103

These are only representative examples; there are many more.

Of special concern are those words where the vowel change needs to be made not only smoothly but *distinctly*.

Some examples:

16–2

b[ea]tific	Mach[ia]vellian
b[ia]s	mall[ea]ble
c[oa]gulate	N[ea]nderthal
cr[ea]ted	noncompl[ia]nt
cr[yi]ng	p[io]neer
d[ia]gram	pr[ea]mble
f[ie]ry	r[ea]listic
g[ia]nt	sc[ie]ntific
h[ia]tus	s[éa]nce
insouc[ia]nt	subsid[ia]ry
l[iai]son	ten[uo]us

The same principle applies to *prefixes*:

16–3

ant[i-a]ircraft	pr[e-e]xisting
c[o-o]perate	pr[o-a]ctive
d[e-e]mphasize	pr[o-A]merican
pr[e-e]mpt	r[e-e]nter

Record these examples. Make sure as you listen to yourself on playback that the change between vowels is very clear and apparent in the examples that call for it.

Chapter Seventeen

Understanding and Interpreting the Script

The Message

Very few scripts present the voice over artist with a phrase or sentence he or she hasn't heard in real life, often many times. The voice over artist *draws* from that experience. Just because it sits there written on a page doesn't mean that the thought process for delivering it should be any different from what you've experienced in real life.

An amazing number of people read aloud without knowing the *meaning* of what they are reading. Many read in a droning mode that elicits little or no effect on the listener. Moreover, many corporate CEOs and politicians have the ability to mesmerize an audience as they speak spontaneously, but the minute they begin to read from a script, some emotionally turn to stone by comparison.

It is absolutely vital that you fully *understand* the script before you deliver one word of it. If it is a particularly difficult, industry-specific, technical, or medical script, then at least try to get a *general* sense of it. If you know, for example, that the solution in beaker A must be poured into beaker B and then heated to form a thick, jellied solution, it doesn't matter that sodium carbonate is in beaker A and phenolphthalein is in beaker B. You have a sense of what is going on in the process and can transmit that to the listener. Pronunciation of these terms can be picked up from the producer and notated phonetically.

Billboarding

It is also very important to know and keep in mind what the primary *subject* of the script is, as well as secondary subjects. For example, consider doing a script about *hotels*:

> "If you're ever in Chicago for a few days, you'll need to stay in a comfortable hotel (secondary subject) to wind down from all that stress you've been under. And where will you find it? At our Embassy Suites Hotel (primary subject)."

In the first sentence, *hotel* is established as the *secondary* subject. In the second sentence, *Embassy Suites* is established as the *primary* subject. Give great weight to these specific words as you read these sentences, since you are establishing your subject for the entire script. This act of giving weight to key subjects is sometimes referred to as *billboarding*. Billboarding sets a subject off and gives it strong theatrical prominence.

If you have a subject that carries throughout a script, the first time the subject is stated, by all means, billboard it. In most cases, when you repeat it at the end of a script, you billboard it again. It's a kind of recap. In the middle of the script, however, you treat it as a redundancy and therefore with no emphasis. If it's a hyped-up promotional or sales piece, often you will billboard it a second or third time.

Here are several more examples of billboarding that you can listen to and work on with the audio:

17–1

> "Solder is a metal alloy."

> "Terminally ill patients need our understanding and support."

"Thomas <u>Jefferson</u> was one of our most revered presidents."

"Our story is about a carefully, patiently built corporation that has succeeded far beyond Wall Street expectations; its name is <u>Danaher</u>."

"<u>Boat building</u> is still popular in the central coastal Maine area."

"As a small business owner, it is important for you to know the benefits of belonging to your chapter of the <u>US Chamber of Commerce</u>."

"If you visit <u>Washington, DC</u>, you'll want to spend an enjoyable evening at the <u>Kennedy</u> Center."

"This week, at <u>Thompson Toyota</u>, we're offering all our models with a super-low-cost three-year warranty!"

Here's another example containing a <u>primary</u> and a <u>secondary</u> subject. Both are emphasized.

"Antique <u>cars</u> (secondary subject) became Harry's obsession, especially his old <u>Dusenberg</u> (primary subject)."

Billboarding is also used to set off *features* and *benefits* of many products, especially *automobiles*.

<u>17–2</u>

"You'll get great <u>driving excitement</u> (benefit) from the newly designed <u>power train</u> (feature). Add to this a <u>cabin interior</u> (feature) that has a custom-designed <u>sound system</u> (feature). The <u>ride</u> (benefit) is cushioned by a reengineered <u>suspension</u> (feature)."

Dramatic Construction of the Message

Almost all sentences end with a bang; that is, the energy builds to a climax. There may be a high point in the middle, but nearly always, the ending, especially *the last word*, is the strongest hit in the sentence. That word also happens to be a *noun* most of the time, although it may be another part of speech as well.

When you read even the shortest sentence, ease into it and keep your vocal energy in reserve to hit on a big ending. The natural tendency for people new to voice over technique is to run out of gas by the time they get to the end of a sentence and almost cavalierly throw it away, when instead the *opposite* effect should occur. Ease into the sentence in the beginning, increase your energy gradually as your progress through the sentence, and give a strong dramatic push to the ending. Note that the listener always has a tendency to remember best the *last* word spoken, not the first. This dramatic push should be especially strong at the end of a topic, before a transition, and most of all, at the end of the entire script itself. Aim for a solid finish with *follow-through*.

Remember that the strongest ending of all is the ending of *the last sentence in the script*. Give this ending a sense of *finality* and *closure* by delivering it with strong focus, intensity, and purpose.

17–3

"I came, I <u>saw</u>, I <u>conquered</u>."

"As he slowly climbed the <u>stairs</u>, he could sense the <u>creature approaching</u> him." (Two builds in a row.)

"The one thing he sought from his cold, aloof <u>father</u> was <u>appreciation</u>."

"No other trip <u>abroad</u> moved me as much as my time in <u>Paris</u>." (Two builds in a row.)

Let the sentence build gradually. Start with low intensity and build to a strong ending.

"As the man thought about his dangerous <u>predicament</u>, to <u>rescue</u> himself, he knew he needed to do something <u>drastic</u>."

If a sentence begins with a noun, particularly the subject of the sentence, the paragraph, or the entire script, it should be emphasized to call attention to it.

"Philo <u>Farnsworth</u> is credited with inventing <u>television</u>."

As I mentioned earlier, a sentence may reach a high point somewhere in the middle, but this does not negate the need for a big ending. To repeat, most high points of emphasis in sentences occur on nouns, but they can also be on intransitive verbs (verbs without an object), transitive verbs with a pronoun as direct object, modifiers (adjectives or adverbs), and, infrequently, other parts of speech. *Nouns*, however, head the list, as I will discuss further in the chapter on "Grama-Drama."

Relative Emphasis

Every verbal communication, every sentence, contains one or several specific words (mostly *nouns*), each of which calls for emphasis for dramatic effect, unless they are *redundant*. However, this emphasis will not be the same for each of these words. You must consider the *emotional weight* of these significant words relative to each other within the framework of the *message*. As you listen to the examples on audio throughout this book, observe this phenomenon. Take note of this also in spontaneous, highly motivated conversation, where the person speaking is totally immersed in his or her subject.

Delivering the Message

Remember, every subject—baseball, waste disposal, war, stamp collecting, accounting, politics, medicine, engineering, antiques, dressmaking, roller coasters, to name just a few—is important to *someone*.

Keep in mind that you have an *objective*. You have *intent, resolve*. You must emotionally support, uphold, and endorse everything you are conveying to the listener.

A word about *medical* and *technical* scripts: try to envision a scenario where you are sitting in a chair and speaking to approximately eight people, who are in a semicircle about six to eight feet in front of you. For a voice over delivery, this is an intimate equivalent to speech delivery in a classroom or lecture hall situation. You must not project as you would in a large room.

Once you fully understand the message, how do you go about communicating it to the listener? There are a number of considerations that will help you deliver your message with maximum effect.

Controlling Your Energy

Every sentence, clause, and phrase should begin with a no-emphasis lead-in. The *energy* at the beginning is low; at the end it is high. The phrase, clause, or sentence should end with a strong declarative emphasis. This also applies to *every time there is a phrasing break in the sentence interior*. Remember, this refers to *emotional energy*, not *volume*. Everything builds, from the shortest phrases to clauses to lists.

Most importantly, don't move outside the emotional energy and pitch parameters you have set for yourself for delivering a particular script.

Know Where You Are

You must keep track of where you are in the script as it unfolds. For the sake of drama, you must be in the moment, but it is also vital to be aware of what lies ahead and, especially, to be mindful of what has come *before*. (See "Redundancy and Reiteration.")

If you're having trouble understanding what's going on in the sentence, delineate who or what is acting (the subject), what the action is (the verb), who or what is the *object* of the action (direct object), and where the action is going (prepositional phrases). Look ahead, but you must also remember what nouns were established earlier in the script, as they will now be *redundant*.

Key Reminder: Never throw away an *ending* except in a *colloquial phrase*, *passive voice*, or a *redundancy*.

17–4

"There is one <u>voice</u> that speaks for all of us who want justice and <u>fairness</u>: the <u>Nation</u>."

"I watched him grow from <u>childhood</u> to become a great <u>man</u>."

(Colloquial phrase, passive voice, and redundancy examples will be given later in the ensuing chapters.)

On Stage vs. In the Studio

Many actors who interpret well on stage have great difficulty with the *intimate* nature of voice over. Acting on stage demands *projection*, often to fifty or more rows of seats. There is a minimal sound level requirement that an actor cannot dip below; otherwise, the message, or part of it, will be lost because of the considerable distance between actor and audience. Sound attenuates (decays) quickly in air.

In the studio, however, the microphone sits six to ten inches away from the actor; it's not unlike speaking into someone's ear. This obviously has intimate, emotional possibilities. Through the playback speakers, the effect to the listener is still intimate, as if the actor is talking to him or her one-on-one. In a large auditorium, the playback system can be turned up much higher in volume to fill the room with sound, but the psychological effect remains the same: an intimate delivery of the message, amplified to fill the room. I call this *amplified intimacy*.

There are, of course, variations on the degree of intimacy, consistent with the message. If the actor is interpreting a sexy cosmetic spot or narrating an emotional event, both scripts suggest an up-close, softer approach to the microphone. Alternatively, one can move away from intimacy incrementally by increasing the distance from the microphone and combining that distance with differing degrees of animation (pitch variations and timbre of the voice) as appropriate. In descending order of intimacy, it might go like this, for example (the distances in feet are those the listener perceives):

17–5

"I love you, Martha." (1 to 2 ft.)

"Could you please pass the salt?" (4 to 8 ft.)

"Throw me the screwdriver before you come down off that ladder." (8 to 14 ft.)

"As soon as the traffic goes by, I'll cross over and join you." (50 to 100 ft.)

In a voice over environment, all these messages are spoken at a distance of a few inches from the microphone. The perceived distance by the listener, however, is produced by a combination of good acting and a good sense of how to create the effect in microcosm. Listen to how this works on the audio track.

To sum it all up, don't project. It's not going to the last row in a theater.

Identification of Listener and Speaker

Always have someone in mind to whom you will deliver the message. Often, a very specific identification of that person is important to the effectiveness of your delivery. Likewise, it is very useful to identify your role as the speaker.

If the message is "This is a great car for a lot of good reasons. You should buy it," you might picture yourself as the car salesman, the owner of the dealership, or the head of the team that designed it. The listener can be someone you just met or someone you know well. He or she could be in any age category, profession, or walk of life.

For instance, if you were narrating a script about child abuse, you might imagine yourself as a psychiatrist, a clinical psychologist, or a social worker. Your listener for this communication could be a parent who is a potential abuser, other professionals like you, or anyone who best fits the image of the perceived target of the message. The choices you make, for both your character and the person to whom you are directing the message, will dramatically affect the way the message comes across.

Reality

Live the experience. Close your eyes and mentally put yourself into whatever the script dictates. Everything you have experienced in life that you can relate to will only add to your effectiveness. No matter how fanciful or phony the script may appear, for you it must be *reality*—or a *pretended* reality. For that brief time, *believe* it!

Reaction

Your emotional reaction may or may not be contrived, depending on how much or how little a specific topic moves you. One thing is certain: if you don't react to it appropriately as you deliver it, neither will the listener. Convince yourself that your message is of vital importance. Ultimately, reaction to events in a speech or script, or anywhere else in real life, stems from human considerations: sympathy, empathy, pleasure, anger, pride, confidence, and so on. You must sound *motivated*, *interested*, and *committed* to your subjects and events. Be *active*, not *passive*. Be *involved*. And remember to take the *script* seriously; don't take *yourself* seriously. It's not about you; it's about the *message*.

The Reality of Playback

Many beginners have a strong tendency to underact (some to extremes) when reading from copy. When we are new to voice over, there is always some degree of self-consciousness since we are working with someone else's thoughts and words. Immediately after the copy is read and recorded, for example, a typical response by an inexperienced reader to his or her performance may be very positive. Indeed, he or she may believe that the performance was worthy of an eight or nine on a scale of one to ten. On playback of the take, however, the actor may realize that the performance was closer to a three or four. This is often due to the fear of overacting. In reality, the reader must record what seems like an *overdone* performance (somewhat equivalent to a thirteen or fourteen) to achieve the desired result. Once the actor makes the connection between what he or she recorded and his or her *actual* performance on playback and corrects the difference, further improvement in performance will begin to happen.

Focus

The intensity of the message generally will determine the degree of *focus* required of the voice over actor. Focus describes the ability to mentally and *visually* concentrate on the activity described by the script, sometimes so much so that the listener will feel that you are looking him or her in the eye as you speak. If you create that scenario between you and the listener in your mind, it will add immeasurably to your effectiveness.

If you are not naturally comfortable delivering verbally serious, intense messages, using *anger* will help you focus. Anger is an emotion that is very specific, as it is directed at someone, something, or most of all, ourselves—a very powerful emotion. After you listen disappointedly to a playback of what you wished to be a focused, dark performance, use anger to get you there. Increase it by degrees, take by take, and listen to each take. Then assess each result until you are where you want to be. A good coach can help you with this approach.

Making Mistakes

Corrections or mistakes can throw off your mental setup for the script. Don't get exasperated when you make a mistake. Simply calmly correct it and stay within the parameters you have set for this script. You must not allow mistakes to unnerve you and throw you off. Expect them and prepare for them. Mistakes may also make you *rush*.

The Pedestal Effect

"I know everything; you know nothing."

The quote above may seem arrogant; it *is*. Just like focus and anger, confidence and arrogance are closely related. When you are in the early learning stages, you will probably need a healthy amount of arrogance to give credibility to your role as spokesperson.

This is especially applicable to teaching or informational situations. You must, as spokesperson, sound as if you are the expert. You are the teacher in the classroom, standing at the blackboard, and it's show-and-tell time. Assume the listener knows nothing. You may have to overdo it for a while, but check your results via playback as you experiment with arrogance incrementally to achieve a confident delivery.

Always assume that what you have to say will have great impact on your audience. You have strong motivation to communicate your message, and your listener is highly motivated to pay attention.

Savor the Moment

It is always critically important to look ahead in the script to prepare for what is to come. However, all the drama is *here and now*, and your main concentration must be in the immediate present, as if in a series of streams of consciousness. It is almost as if your mind is a wandering emotional magnet that attaches itself to everything to which it relates.

With this in mind, immerse yourself in the following script, rich in contemplation and reflection. If it's appropriate, substitute *John* for *Joan*. Get into it. Identify with the person in the script. *Be* that person. *Savor* each moment in time, each stream of consciousness. Then, listen to how it's done on the audio track.

115

17–6

"I look at the beauty of the rocky coastline surrounding the cottage; it's been in my family for four generations. The red sunset still warms my face, even though the sun is almost down. Life has been good to me. For thirty years Joan and I have been together, and we're still in love. Every summer here at the Cape is a constant reassurance that everything is as I want it to be. I'm very lucky."

Be Comfortable

As you read a script, sit or stand comfortably, as you prefer, and breathe calmly and quietly through your mouth and nose. Your mouth should move minimally, and without tension. Speak in a normal conversational tone; *don't force anything.*

In contrast with the relaxed condition of the body, your mind should be cooking with gas. Aware. Spirited. Receptive. *Alert.*

Remember these steps:

- One idea—one event—at a time.
- Take your time, and pause at every logical opportunity.
- Think ahead as you go. Be aware of what comes next.
- The script is only a roadmap for spoken communication— thoughts becoming verbalized.
- *Talk* to your listener; don't read.

Remember also that what you are narrating will be embellished by moving visuals, music, and sometimes sound effects. Imagine and allow for them in your read.

Read vs. Talk Considerations

When we speak of a highly motivating experience or event, it is usually with a great deal of mental energy, enthusiasm, and certainly focus.

We are totally absorbed in the subject and in relating the experience to someone else. The subject could be a trip to Europe, a new car, a strong opinion, a reminiscence—the list is endless. We are seeking a reaction from the listener that mirrors our own feelings about the subject or event we are describing. As we share the event, we are making an effort to persuade the listener to side with us.

When we interpret a script, the process is similar. For the voice over artist, the script is a road map for live, one-on-one communication. It is simply the supply source of message material—a message to be delivered, to be communicated to someone else, and it must be done with a purposeful, conversational focus, as if you were looking the listener straight in the eye as you speak. The more intense the subject, the more intense the look.

The process of conveying an impression of spontaneity with a message written by someone other than the speaker is a *contrivance*. Therefore, the art of voice over interpretation might well be called *contrived spontaneity*. Since you are working with a message that is essentially someone else's, you must find a way to make it *your* message. If there is one ideal goal for the voice over artist, it is to bring together the *contrived* self and the *spontaneous* self. With the best voice over artists, these selves are indistinguishable.

Delivering in Statements

The following is a reiteration of a basic principle, stated earlier in this chapter, that you must always remember when delivering any script. Commit this principle to memory and make good use of it, no matter what kind of voice over work you are doing:

Every sentence, every clause, every phrase should begin with a weak beat and, most of the time, a low note. The energy at the beginning is low; at the end it is high. Everything in between the two *builds*. The phrase, clause, or sentence should end with a strong declarative emphasis. This also applies to *every phrasing break in the sentence interior*. Each part should be considered as an individual declarative sentence by itself. Remember, this refers to *emotional* energy, not *volume*. Everything builds, from the shortest *phrases* to *clauses* to *lists*.

Exceptions to the above are as follows (using a *strong* beat, as opposed to a weak beat at the beginning):

17–7

1. If it begins with a *noun*
   "Thomas Jefferson was one of our first presidents."
   "Paris is my favorite city."

2. If it begins with an *exclamation*
   "Wow, look at that iceberg!"
   "Gosh, I had no idea you liked me more than just as a friend."

3. If it begins with a *transitional adverb*
   "Finally, after all this time, we meet."
   "However, after listening to your side of the story, I disagree."

4. If it begins with a *one-word setting*
   "Yesterday, I went to the movies."
   "Today, I stayed home."
   "Tomorrow, I'm going to the supermarket."

5. If it begins with a *demonstrative pronoun*
   "This is paradise."
   "These are the men and women of network sports."

To illustrate how the beginnings of most sentences should be read, the following examples serve to demonstrate the low-note weak-beat beginnings of phrases and clauses. Listen carefully to the difference between the wrong and right approaches on the audio tracks:

17–8

"On a beautiful fall night in 1968…"

"When I was a young man…"

"Sensing his opponent's weaknesses…"

"There were many angry words exchanged between the two women…"

"Before the man realized what was happening…"

The next examples carry the low-note weak-beat concept further. In each of these examples, the beginning of every subsequent phrase or clause in the sentence is delivered the same as the opening phrase or clause, illustrated by parentheses:

17–9

"(Even if you lose), (being in the game will be worth the experience)."

"(As he felt his comrade dying in his arms), (the battle-weary soldier wept uncontrollably)."

"(If you're going to make your mark in this world), (you need to work hard) (and doggedly persist) (in pursuit of your goals.)"

"(It was bitterly cold) (on the morning of Election Day 1932), (and the turnout was far below expectations)."

"(Just before sunup), (the raiding party made its final preparations) (for the attack)."

Be sure to take note of the focus on the *nouns*, as the sentences unfold.

Understanding how these phrases and clauses operate individually and how they relate to the entire sentence is critical to the perceived spontaneity of your delivery. You must sound to the listener as if every phrase and clause you utter is coming from your own stream of consciousness. It must sound natural, evenly paced, and smooth. Most importantly, it must make recurrent use of *pauses*, as they enhance the dramatic effect far more than you may realize.

For me, this is the single most fundamental section of this book. Come back to it often, review it, and practice it, until the concept becomes automatic.

Why We Read Aloud the Way We Do

How many times have you listened to a lay reader in church or witnessed a reading-aloud event by a high school or college student? For a very high percentage of those times, the reader delivers the lines in droning phrases that seem to anticipate the phrase that follows the one being read, and no one ever ends anything in a *statement* until he or she comes to a period. That is how nearly all of us read aloud, from childhood to the grave.

On the other hand, when people *talk*, every phrase, clause, and sentence nearly always ends in a *statement*. This is because people talk mostly in *statements*. In other words, nearly every time there is a phrasing pause, it ends in a statement, not an anticipatory hanging inflection. This conveys a sense of *purpose* and *focus* to every event within, or at the end of, virtually every phrase, clause, and sentence. Even individual words get a declarative treatment in some situations, which greatly enhances the drama. Unfortunately, "upspeak" is now part of everyday language in some social orders, as in "Valley-Girl talk." This is not recommended for voice over delivery, except for character imitation.

Now let's look at stage and film acting for a moment. Some of us took some theater courses in high school and college. A few went on to more serious professional pursuits in the theater arts. However, the theater experience did not address the reading-out-loud-from-copy issue.

In the theater, the first rehearsal of a play usually involves a *read-through* of the script, some discussions about the nature of the characters in the script, the overall feel of the play, and so on. Then each member of the cast goes home, reads the script over and over, and then *memorizes* his or her lines. When the actors later begin rehearsal, every line that is delivered, from rehearsal to final performance, is spoken to another actor or delivered as a soliloquy. The actor is given a great deal of expressive freedom, stemming from the fact that he or she has memorized the lines. Every line mimics everyday verbal communication from one person to another. Even the *visual* imagery of the delivery is there, and it is *live*.

Therein lies the major difference between stage acting and voice over acting. The actor memorizes and delivers the lines, live, to other actors or to the audience. The voice over actor does not benefit from having memorized the lines, because the voice over session is a one-time event, and the economies of scale do not lend themselves to memorization. He or she usually delivers lines to a microphone with no one else in the room (unless it is a multiperson script, which is rare). There may be a small audience sitting behind a control room window in a studio setting, or the voice actor may be alone in his or her home studio. It's a stark environment when you consider that a stage actor works on a set with a live audience and is there with other actors to whom he or she can deliver lines in a realistic scenario. For the film actor, it's even more vivid, since the settings are often much more elaborate.

In a studio environment, however, the voice over actor needs to possess a very fertile *imagination*, as visual images suggested by the script must be fantasized and experienced as if real. In addition, he or she must conjure up a visualized *delivery scenario*, wherein the person to whom the lines are spoken is actually seen and reacted to in the actor's imagination. To clarify, the voice over actor uses *two sets* of visual imagery—experiencing the visual and situational events described in the script and speaking the message to a live listener.

A major contributing element to the droning effect is the reader's detachment from the *message*. We have all picked up this habit by

121

enduring boring classroom situations where we were called on to read aloud, and in the process of doing it, we focused entirely on pronouncing the words correctly and on our own performances. We didn't think about the *meaning* of the pieces we were reading. Consequently, most of us learned to read aloud while our brains were on hold, unable to break down the real message and deliver it to our audience. This is a very common phenomenon.

People who *read* only look *ahead* and *think* ahead. People who *talk* also look *back* and remember the subjects that have already been introduced. They keep track and have a sense of *context*.

Now let's further examine the droning effect. When people read, they are always anticipating what comes next, and consequently, words, phrases, and clauses are delivered in hanging inflections, as if all the elements were in one never-ending list. The only times the reader truly *ends* these elements is when he or she comes to a *period*. Thus, the reader can make the assumption that the only real *declaration* is at the end of the entire sentence. When people *talk*, a very different scenario unfolds. Each *event* in a sentence has its own ending. In many sentences, there can be *several* events with solid endings, because people talk in declarative *streams of consciousness*. In other words, every event in a sentence is delivered as a *statement*. Instead of one long droning sentence with one ending, a sentence is broken up into shorter segments that make one assertion after another, with very few exceptions.

On the audio tracks accompanying this book, the following sentences are delivered both as if *reading* and then, in contrast, as if *talking*:

17–10

"I went to a movie. After a couple of hours, I came home and puttered around the house. Then, later on, I left for my date with Cynthia."

17–11

"It is the bedrock of our beliefs—the heart, the brain, the very soul of our existence."

17–12

"He was accused of using slave labor to construct the huge complex—Hungarian gypsies from a concentration camp—as carriers and pullers for the heavy equipment."

17–13

"They looked out over the vast reaches of the mountain range and at the sun slowly disappearing behind it. This is where we want to be for the rest of our lives, they thought."

17–14

"The young officer is in full uniform, as if on parade. He is all agleam with bullion—a blue and gold edition of the Poetry of War. A wave of derisive laughter runs abreast of him all along the line. But how handsome he is!—with what careless grace he sits his horse!" (Ambrose Bierce, *Civil War Stories*)

17–15

"Plastic cups, beer and soda cans, garnishing highways. Miles and miles of seemingly unending floating junk, clinging to islands in the middle of the Pacific. Block after block of uninhabitable slums in cities. Vast oil slicks on the surface, and clinging to the bottoms, of bays and oceans. Cutoff mountaintops, dug out for coal. Poisoned waterways. The list goes on.

"These are man's devastations. With his ravenous hunger for wealth and prosperity, he uses, exploits, and discards. In one reckless act after another, he lays waste the earth, as he inexorably satiates himself, never considering for a moment that the riches of Planet

Earth are disappearing, as death by a thousand cuts, never to return."
(John Burr, *Indelible Footprints*)

17–16

"With malice toward none; with charity for all; with firmness in the right, as God gives us to see the right, let us strive on to finish the work we are in; to bind up the nation's wounds; to care for him who shall have borne the battle, and for his widow, and his orphan—to do all which may achieve and cherish a just and lasting peace, among ourselves, and with all nations." (Abraham Lincoln)

17–17

"In the beginning God created the heaven and the earth. And the earth was without form, and void; and darkness was upon the face of the deep. And the spirit of God moved upon the face of the waters. And God said, 'Let there be light'; and there was light." (Genesis 1:1–3)

Do you hear the difference between the reading and talking versions? The reading versions are dispassionate and boring. The talking versions have purpose and focus. They evoke reality.

Imitation

Imitation is a very significant component of the learning process, not only as it applies to voice over delivery but in other artistic areas as well.

Writers learn to write by imitating other writers' styles. Artists learn to paint by imitating other artists' styles and brush techniques. Composers learn by imitating other composers.

The idea is not to turn your delivery into a clone of the style you're imitating but to enable you to use some of that style and merge it with a portion of other styles learned by imitating *other* sources. Thus, the style of a Hemingway, a Picasso, or a Stravinsky is formed by a *combination* of the styles they have learned by imitating their accomplished peers, and they have made conscious or unconscious choices as to how little or how much of each source to incorporate into their own creative mixes. The voice over student learns in the same way. Avail yourself of every opportunity to seriously analyze and imitate people whose styles you admire. You will discover that many of these styles will not be a good fit for you, but several will be. You will discover in time how much of each you want to retain to create your *own* combination, hence, your own *style*.

Movement of the Hands and Body

Several voice coaches advocate using a good measure of body language to support an effective delivery, including a standing delivery, as opposed to sitting. My opinion is that you should do whatever is comfortable for you. I have observed voice actors over the last thirty years in my own studios, and among the sitters and the standers, I observed solid delivery skills from both.

With regard to use of the hands, I do believe that some overt gesturing is beneficial. However, a number of my students came to the table with a propensity for using their hands in time with the points of emphasis, which resulted in a very uneven, choppy delivery, as well as an inconsistent level.

In these situations, I always recommended folding one's hands to prevent continuation of this habit. Following this correction, there will be a strong urge to move the hands as you read, but over time, this will diminish. Every time I have directed a student to do this, there has been an immediate change in the smoothness of the delivery.

Once the student is able to deliver without moving his or her hands in time with the rhythm of the script, then we can focus on using the hands in a general way for dramatic effect.

Another point about hands is this: do not follow along with a pencil or finger on the script as you deliver it. This is by its very nature a mechanical act, and it will distract you from using your imagination and from communicating directly with your listener.

Directability

We've talked about the many ways to make your interpretations sizzle. Then one day, you walk into a studio or do a phone patch or Skype session in your home studio with someone with whom you've never worked. As you move through the session, you receive many corrections from the producer or director that run contrary to your own instincts or to many of the concepts that I've described in this book. So what do you do?

The short answer to this is that you do *everything the way you are instructed to do it* by the producer or director. I've already said several times that a lot of voice over talents in the business don't understand many of the observations in this book. Unfortunately, neither do some *producers and directors*. However, he or she is either the person who hired you or the representative for the company who hired you. Hence, it is the producer or director's right to ask to have the script interpreted the way he or she *wants* it interpreted. Be professional. If you are courteous and flexible and do a good job, you will be pleasantly remembered for it and will probably be hired again. Keep in mind that not every project using your voice will necessarily be something you'll want to put on your demo, but it's incumbent upon you to accommodate every direction you receive.

Here's a fun exercise to hone your imitative skills, especially when a client wants you to emphasize in places that go against your instincts. Follow the underlines. You can also listen to this on the audio track:

17–18

(No emphasis)   "This stuff is really good!"

(With emphasis, as underlined)   "This <u>stuff</u> is really <u>good</u>!"
                                                  "<u>This</u> stuff is <u>really</u> good!"
                                                  "This stuff <u>is</u> really good!"
                                                  "<u>This</u> <u>stuff</u> <u>is</u> <u>really</u> <u>good</u>!"

Not as easy as it looks, is it?

One final tip: be a careful reader. Read only the words as they appear in the script. Don't put in what *isn't*; don't take out what *is*.

Finally, if you see something in the script that you feel should be changed or eliminated, you may ask the producer if he or she thinks your point is valid only after you have assessed whether or not the producer or director seems flexible. If there is any doubt at all, leave it alone. Do as you're asked to do. That's the professional way.

Chapter Eighteen
GRAMA-DRAMA: HOW WORDS INTERACT

Grammar is a piano I play by ear. All I know about grammar is its power.

—Joan Didion (1934–present)
American Journalist and Novelist

No area of performance confounds the voice over artist more than figuring out which words in a script should be emphasized and which need no emphasis. It is almost impossible to learn how to do this without a reasonable mastery of English-language dynamics.

It is probably not an exaggeration to state that most people don't know very much about parts of speech or grammar in general, for that matter, and certainly not enough to do *narrations* and *audiobooks* effectively. I remember reading recently that over *80 percent* of adults in the United States could not pass a fifth-grade English final exam.

Within this framework, it is very important that you understand and can identify parts of speech, recognize their individual functions, and know where and why to *emphasize* and *not* to emphasize.

I call this *Grama-Drama.*

We begin with *nouns.*

Nouns are persons, places, or things (right out of English 101). In this business, nouns are also *pictures*. When we deliver any message, it is filled with pictures of *some person, some place, or some thing*. We are conjuring up *images* for our audience.

Since these images are vital to audience reaction, it follows that to make them appealing to the listener, we need to give them *emphasis*. Nouns are emphasized more than any other part of speech.

Where do nouns appear in sentences? They appear as *subjects* (those that do the action), objects of *verbs* (that which is acted upon by the subject via the verb), and objects of *prepositions* (led to by position, time, or direction).

Here's a simple example:

18–1

"John rode the <u>bus</u> to the <u>theater</u>." *John* is the subject. *Bus* is the object of the verb *rode*, or the action. *Theater* is the object of the preposition *to*.

Here's another example:

"In the tiny <u>kitchen</u>, <u>Sarah</u> made a tasty <u>omelet</u> for her <u>boyfriend</u>."

Here, *Sarah* is the subject. *Omelet* is the object of the verb m*ade*. There are two prepositional phrases. *Kitchen* is the object of the preposition *in*. *Boyfriend* is the object of the preposition *for*.

Who is doing the action? *Sarah*.

What is being acted upon? *Omelet*.

Where is this happening? The *kitchen*.

For whom is the omelet made? Her *boyfriend*.

The sentence may also be constructed with boyfriend as an *indirect* object:

"In the tiny <u>kitchen</u>, <u>Sarah</u> made her boyfriend a tasty <u>omelet</u>." (As an indirect object, *boyfriend* is not emphasized.)

Close your eyes mentally and visualize Sarah, the omelet, the kitchen, and her boyfriend—all *pictures*. Sarah is making an omelet. Making the omelet is the *action*. More about this when we get to *verbs*.

Distinguishing a noun from any other part of speech is really quite simple. Put an article—*a* or *the*—in front of the word in question, and if it makes sense to you, it's a noun. This does not apply to names of *people* or *places* (proper nouns).

Very heavy emotional emphasis is appropriate for a noun that is the subject of an entire script or is especially significant to the script or a subtopic within the script. Many in this business call this *billboarding*. Billboarding is simply giving emotional weight to a word that is significantly important to a sentence, a paragraph, or an entire script. Billboarding is discussed in greater detail in "Understanding and Interpreting the Script."

Here are some examples of billboarding nouns:

18–2

"The American <u>Cancer</u> Society needs your help."

"Thomas <u>Jefferson</u> was one of our greatest presidents."

"WKT<u>C</u>. Giving you breaking news, as it happens." (Note that the emphasis is on the <u>last</u> call letter, *C*.)

"Junk <u>food</u> is very popular in America."

Note that billboarding applies to words that are stated for the *first time* only. (See "Redundancy and Reiteration.")

Collective nouns describe a group, though the noun itself is singular. Typical collective nouns are *committee, family, furniture*, and *equipment*.

Verbs can act as nouns. They are called *gerunds*.

Infinitives can also act as nouns.

18–3

"<u>Swimming</u> is the healthiest of all sports." (gerund)
To <u>swim</u> is to be doing what I love best. (infinitive)
"<u>Knowing</u> her is to dislike her intensely." (gerund)
To <u>know</u> her is to dislike her intensely. (infinitive)
"The name of the game is <u>winning</u>." (gerund)

To win is the name of the game. (infinitive)

As with nouns, they are *emphasized* in these situations.

Proper Nouns

Proper nouns always begin with a capital letter, unlike *common nouns*, which begin with a lowercase letter. *Proper* nouns describe particular people, very specific places, and groups or events. They are always *capitalized*.

Typical proper nouns include, for example, George Washington (person), London (place), the Federal Aviation Administration (group), and the Super Bowl (event). With proper names like George <u>Washington</u>, the emphasis is always on the *surname* (the last name only).

The following are examples of proper nouns with common nouns that relate to them.

18–4

Proper noun:	Common noun:
Everest	mountain
Frank	man/boy
Mississippi	river
Pacific	ocean
Spain	country

18–5

Proper nouns as *places*:	As *schools and colleges*:
Bangor, <u>Maine</u>	Columbia Community <u>College</u>
Paris, <u>France</u>	Harvard <u>University</u>
Toronto, Ontario, <u>Canada</u>	Riverview <u>Academy</u>
Washington, <u>DC</u>	Rock Creek <u>High</u> School
West Wappinger Falls, New <u>York</u>	The <u>Hill</u> School

18–6

As *street names*:	As *organizations*:
Barclay <u>Square</u>	<u>Alzheimer's</u> Association
Bradley <u>Boulevard</u>	Arts <u>Alliance</u>
Gramercy <u>Court</u>	<u>Founders'</u> Club
<u>Main</u> Street	<u>Humane</u> Society
Meridian <u>Circle</u>	National <u>Science</u>
Merritt <u>Parkway</u>	Foundation
<u>Park</u> Place	
Penny <u>Lane</u>	
River <u>Bend</u>	
Tamiami <u>Trail</u>	
Ventnor <u>Avenue</u>	
Wofford <u>Way</u>	

Proper nouns as *names* need special consideration:

18–7

John <u>Smith</u>

John Alden <u>Smith</u>

John Jacob Jingleheimer <u>Smith</u>

Note that in all groupings of names and places, the point of emphasis is *always* placed on the last word when the proper noun is initially introduced, as that final word is always the destination. In the case of names, the emphasis will be on the *surname*.

If we add a *title* to a proper noun (usually a proper name), the same rule applies. There's no emphasis until the final destination—the last word.

18–8

Sir Charles <u>Dinwiddie</u>

General Ulysses S. <u>Grant</u>

The English writer Charles <u>Dickens</u>

Secretary of State William <u>Stanton</u>

Chief Justice of the Supreme Court John <u>Roberts</u>

The historic city of <u>London</u>

London Gainsborough painting restoration specialist Nigel <u>Booth</u>

As I said earlier, these rules apply to when the proper noun is *initially introduced*. Once the person or place is established, the last word is treated as a *redundancy* and therefore is not emphasized. (See "Redundancy and Reiteration.")

Here is a short example:

18–9

"It was a tragic series of events. Phoebe <u>Nolan</u> was doing her homework alone in her bedroom. But <u>Billy</u> (Nolan) and his wife thought (Phoebe) was staying with her girlfriend that night. They heard noises as they entered the house, so (Billy) grabbed his rifle and moved quickly upstairs to investigate. When he entered (Phoebe's) room, she jumped out at him from the closet. Reacting reflexively, he shot her point-blank in the chest."

The first time *Phoebe* is introduced, the emphasis is on the surname. When *Billy* is introduced, his first name is emphasized, since he is part of the family with the surname *Nolan*. (In this case, we are distinguishing him from her.) For the remainder of the story, *neither* Phoebe nor Billy is emphasized, as they are now established as the subjects of the story.

Verbs

If nouns are the *pictures*, verbs are the *actions*. Verbs can also be expressed as a state of *being*, as in derivatives of the verb *to be*. For our purposes in voice over work, let's consider action verbs to be in two categories: *transitive* and *intransitive*.

A *transitive* verb takes an object, which means that it *acts* on the object. *Trans* means *across* or *through*; therefore, in the case of a transitive verb, the emphasis is placed on the *object*, which is almost always a noun. Since we are traveling through or across the verb, the action is directed to the object.

Here are several examples:

18–10

"Norman washed his <u>car</u> every day."
"I watched Stan <u>Musial</u> as he hit a home run."
"In spite of not being hungry, Alice ate the <u>hot dog</u>."
"With horrifying velocity, the meteor struck the <u>earth</u>."

Be sure to refer to the chapter called "Destinations." The last example is one of the many in which, if turned around, the destination will remove the emphasis from *earth* and take it to *velocity*. Here's the altered version:

"The meteor struck the earth with horrifying <u>velocity</u>." Earth is now no longer emphasized because it is followed by a prepositional phrase.

The verb can also end the sentence, and in that case it is emphasized.

18–11

"The tool is remarkably easy to set up and <u>use</u>."

Here are two more examples, using *pronoun* objects:

"He <u>helped</u> (her) immensely."

"The scientists <u>developed</u> (it) over a long period of time."

Strong Transitive Verbs

Some transitive verbs by nature carry a lot of dramatic weight ("hot" words), and for that reason, even though we still emphasize the object of the verb, we emphasize the dramatic verb, too.

18–12

"Thomas Edison <u>pioneered</u> the development of <u>electricity</u>."

"General Ito <u>committed</u> his <u>troops</u>."

"His creations <u>mesmerized</u> <u>moviegoers</u>."

"Some say Wall Street has <u>spoofed</u> the <u>public</u>."

"The racy dialogue <u>shocked</u> <u>audiences</u>."

"I need to verify your <u>credentials</u>."

Here's another example with a *redundant* object:

18–13

"<u>Property</u> taxes are costly. Many Americans are <u>overpaying</u> their (property taxes) unnecessarily."

Keep in mind that we are illustrating very basic examples of transitive verbs, and there are more developmental situations in which the emphasis on the object can be affected by other factors, such as a prepositional phrase that immediately follows the object.

18–14

"He immediately saw the <u>object</u>. He immediately saw the (object) in the <u>room</u>."

"The second baseman hit the <u>ball</u>. The second baseman hit the (ball) with <u>gusto</u>."

Note also in the above examples that if you consider the two sentences in each example to be in sequence, the second sentence notes that *object* in the first example and *ball* in the second example are redundancies since they were emphasized in each preceding sentence. Hence, they would not be emphasized, because they are redundant.

Intransitive Verbs

An *intransitive* verb is its own action; it does not act on an object. The subject does not go across the verb to act on an object. It simply acts by itself.

Some examples are as follows:

18–15

"Mary <u>cried</u>." (Add an adverb.) "Mary <u>cried profusely</u>."

"Mark loves to <u>read</u>."

"She loved to watch him <u>paint</u>."

The above examples used as *transitive* verbs with *objects* might also read

"Mary cried salty <u>tears</u>."

"Mark loves to read dime <u>novels</u>."

"She loved to watch him paint <u>portraits</u>."

Intransitive verbs can also lead into a prepositional phrase, in which case they are not emphasized.

18–16

> "…while the <u>sun</u> (set) slowly down in the sky."

> "He was (meandering) down a country <u>road</u>."

> "She was (photographed) with an expression of <u>horror</u> on her face."

> "He had many <u>horses</u> that he had (loved) since <u>boyhood</u>."

The prepositional phrases extend the *destination*.

Linking Verbs

Linking verbs are derivations of the verb *to be*. *Am, are, is, was, were, has been, have been, will be, will have been*, and the like are all linking verbs. Linking verbs express a *state of being*, unlike transitive and intransitive verbs that express *action*.

Here are sentences with *no* emphasis on the verbs—the most common use of linking verbs:

18–17

> "Hank (is) my best friend."

> "There (will be) hell to pay for this mistake."

> "If I (were) you, I would leave town now."

Now, here are sentences *with* emphasis on the verbs:

18–18

> "I don't know who these people <u>are</u>, but hopefully you do."

> "She was concerned about where he had <u>been</u>, but she decided not to <u>ask</u> him about it."

Finally, here's a sentence with emphasis on one verb and none on the other:

18–19

"What a giant among men he <u>was</u>, so significant (were) his scientific contributions."

Linking verbs may also function as auxiliary verbs in passive voice and are not emphasized.

18–20

"The speaker (was) introduced by the moderator."

"Every time mention (is) made of my contribution, I try to change the subject."

A few action verbs—*look, taste, smell*—can also be linking verbs, depending on how they are used.

18–21

"He (looked) worn <u>out</u>." (state of being)

"He <u>looked</u> at her strangely." (action)

"The place (smelled) of rotting <u>food</u>." (state of being)

"He (smelled) her <u>perfume</u>." (action)

Gerunds

Remember that verbs can be used as *nouns*, which we refer to as *gerunds*. Gerunds follow the same rules as nouns, in terms of where they should be emphasized. Some examples are as follows:

Swimming, boating, running, jumping, painting, breathing, camping, eating, sleeping, jogging, playing, meeting, keeping, shooting, managing

Remember that gerunds, like regular verbs, can be *transitive* or *intransitive*, although most are *intransitive*.

18–22

Transitive:

> "He made every effort to achieve the goals of the war, without (destroying) the new nation in the process."

Intransitive:

> "Using a common sense ratio, *playing* is as important as *working*."

Participles

A *participle*, for our purposes, is a verb performing as an adjective. It may also take an object or an adverb as modifier. It may be used simply as a solitary *adjective* as in the following examples, with participles in parenthesis:

18–23

> (Singing) <u>sopranos</u>, (known) <u>child</u> molester, (implied) <u>innuendo</u>, (running) <u>candidate</u>

A participle can also be illustrated as an adjective connected with subordinate elements (in parenthesis) in a *participial phrase*:

18–24

> "The <u>sopranos,</u> (singing at the top of their range), filled the hall with joyous song."

> "As a (known) child molester, he kept to <u>himself</u>."

> "His carefully (implied) innuendo made Evelyn <u>uncomfortable</u>."

> "Since Joe was a (front-running) <u>candidate</u>, the <u>election</u> process was <u>window</u> dressing."

Just to remind you, these are verbs operating as adjectives. Apply the emphasis rules as you would for adjectives in the "Adjectives" section of this chapter.

Auxiliary Verbs vs. Principal Verbs

A main verb is called a *principal* verb. It expresses an act or state:

18–25

"I <u>understand</u>."

"I <u>slept</u> last night."

"I <u>help</u> whenever I can."

"Problems <u>arise</u>."

An *auxiliary* verb is used with a principal verb to form a combination that expresses tense, mood, or voice. The auxiliaries are in parenthesis:

18–26

"I (can) <u>understand</u>."

"I (may) <u>read</u> tonight."

"I (will) <u>help</u> you."

"Problems are (going to) <u>arise</u>."

"They (weren't) going through the <u>motions</u>."

In this last case, *going* is the main verb, but it is not emphasized, as it is followed by a prepositional phrase—a destination. (See "Destinations.")

The most common auxiliary verbs are *be, can, do, have, may, must, shall, will, ought, let,* and *going to*.

For our purposes, the important point to remember about auxiliary verbs is that they are *never* emphasized. They exist only in combination with the main, or principal, verbs and are therefore secondary to them. It makes no difference whether or not the principal verb is transitive or intransitive; the auxiliary verb is still not emphasized.

Infinitives

The infinitive has been called a *verbal noun*, in that it is not dependent on a connection with a subject in the way of a normal verb. It is always used in combination with the preposition *to*.

Some examples are as follows:

to <u>have</u>, to <u>know</u>, to <u>help</u>, to <u>love</u>

Infinitives function as transitive or intransitive and are affected by destinations in the same way as principal verbs.

Pronouns

Pronouns are stand-ins for nouns, a guard against redundancy. They are always synonymous with a noun that has been previously introduced or a noun that is *implied* to have been introduced.

The most important point to remember about *all* pronouns is they are almost *never emphasized*. Treat them as low-pitched throwaways as they are, by nature, redundant. The only exception to this rule applies to cases of comparison and contrast, which may also be stated or implied. There is normally no emphasis on pronouns.

Subject Pronouns

I, you, he, she, it, we, they, one (subjects of a verb)

Examples (pronouns in parenthesis):

18–27

"<u>Tony</u> knows exactly what (he) must <u>do</u> about this."

"(I) am in love with <u>Anne</u>."

"(She) is my ideal <u>woman</u>."

"As members of the committee, perhaps (we) should reconsider our position."

"(It) would be a huge mistake to ignore our intuition."

"(One) doesn't interrupt, unless (one) wants to be interrupted."

Object Pronouns

Me, you, him, her, it, us, them, one (objects of a verb, infinitive, or preposition)

18–28

"George <u>insulted</u> (her) constantly."

"Norman's attitude <u>bothered</u> (me)."

"Carol and Sylvia wanted (him) to go to the <u>operation</u> with (them)."

"Joe resolved to give (it) his best <u>shot</u>."

"These are <u>good</u>. <u>Have</u> (one)."

And here's a rhyme version:

"I'm so sorry my zoysia <u>annoys</u> (ya)."

Possessive Pronouns

My, your, his, her, its, our, their (treated as a *preceding modifier*, with no emphasis)

18–29

"This is (my) <u>dog</u>."

"He tried to hold (his) <u>breath</u> for several minutes."

"This thing has taken on a life of (its) <u>own</u>."

"After discussing the accident, we decided that it was (our) <u>fault</u>."

"The chairman couldn't understand (their) <u>inflexibility</u>."

Ownership Pronouns

Mine, yours, his, hers, its, ours, theirs

These answer the question "Whose *is* this?" These are used in comparison/contrast situations and are therefore emphasized.

18–30

"This jewelry is <u>mine</u>."

"Is this package on the shelf <u>yours</u>? Or <u>his</u>?"

"I never dreamed that this house would be <u>ours</u> someday."

"You have <u>your</u> opinion; they have <u>theirs</u>."

The same exception works for *possessive pronouns* previously described: *my, your, his, her,* etc.

"This is <u>my</u> jewelry."

"Does this package on the shelf belong to <u>you</u>?"

"I never dreamed that this house would belong to <u>us</u> someday."

"You have <u>your</u> opinion; they have <u>their</u> opinion."

Here are other exceptions involving implied comparisons (following *to be* verbs):

18–31

"It is <u>I</u> who threw the rock through your window."

(Not someone else.)

"It was <u>they</u> who answered the <u>emergency</u> call."
(Incorrectly, many people use *me* or *them*.)

Relative Pronouns

Who, what, which, whom, whatever, whomever, etc.

These link a subordinate clause to the main clause in the sentence. Again, they are not emphasized.

18–32

"He did not tell me the truth, (which) made me angry."

"Karen went to her doctor, (who) had given her good advice previously."

"She was not certain (whom) she could count on."

"You can take (whatever) you want."

"They told her she could bring (whomever) she wished to the party."

Reflexive Pronouns

Reflexive pronouns are personal pronouns that have the suffix *self* or *selves* added to them. They are called *reflexive* because they reflect back on a previously introduced noun or pronoun for which they stand. As with all pronouns, they are not emphasized except in comparisons or contrasts.

Here are some typical reflexive pronouns as they are used in sentences, with the pronouns in parenthesis:

18–33

"Narcissus admired (himself) in the reflection in the calm water."

"The woman composed (herself) as she tried to recover from the embarrassing remark."

"The artists took pride (in themselves) and their work."

"Now, Billy, behave (yourself)! You don't want to hurt (anyone)."

An interesting exception uses a transitive verb and an object; therefore, the *verb* is not emphasized.

18–34

"The town that calls (itself) <u>home</u> wants to make you feel welcome."

Sometimes, but not often, reflexive pronouns will be emphasized for dramatic effect:

"I <u>myself</u> found her explanation to be questionable."

"The solemnity of the funeral affected the president <u>himself</u>."

"Go ahead. Help <u>yourself</u>."

Reciprocal pronouns

Reciprocal pronouns are described as such because the action of each is perceived as affecting the other. These, too, are not emphasized, as with other pronouns. *Each other* and *one another* constitute the reciprocal pronouns. *Each other* describes two persons; *one another*, more than two.

Here are two examples in sentences; again, pronouns are in parenthesis:

18–35

"The husband and <u>wife</u> looked <u>out</u> for (each other)."

"The <u>Bible</u> says that we should <u>love</u> (one another)."

Interrogative Pronouns

Who, whom, what, which

Interrogative pronouns are used to ask questions (no emphasis, as before).

18–36

"(Who) took my piece of apple <u>pie</u>?"

"(Whom) shall I ask to the <u>prom</u>?"

"(What) was I <u>thinking</u> when I <u>said</u> that?"

"(Which) <u>dog</u> do you want to take <u>home</u>?"

Demonstrative Pronouns

This, these, that, those

Demonstrative pronouns are *point-to* pronouns to identify that which one is describing.

Demonstrative pronouns are other exceptions to the usual rule of no emphasis for pronouns, as they are calling attention to someone, something, or someplace. Again, a comparison or contrast is implied, as you are singling out one from others.

18–37

"<u>This</u> is the best I've ever <u>seen</u>!"

"<u>These</u> are the men and women of our armed <u>forces</u>."

"<u>Those</u> are the lowlifes I <u>told</u> you about."

Here is a demonstrative pronoun not at the beginning of the sentence:

"Now imagine <u>this</u>!"

Indefinite Pronouns

Indefinite pronouns are also emphasized, as they are emphatically making a point.

Singular indefinite pronouns include *each, every, anybody, anything, somebody*, and *something*.

18–38

"<u>Each</u> of the men wanted to be <u>heard</u>."

"Will <u>anybody</u> stand up and be <u>counted</u>?"

"Is <u>anything sacred</u> anymore?"

"There must be <u>something</u> we can do." (In a less dramatic situation, these sentences will work if the indefinite pronouns are *not* emphasized.)

Plural indefinite pronouns include *both, several, few, many,* and *plenty.*

18–39

"<u>Both</u> of the <u>vases</u> were broken."

"<u>Several</u> among the group left <u>early</u>."

"<u>Many</u> are <u>called</u>, but <u>few</u> are <u>chosen</u>."

"I've been to <u>London plenty</u> of times."

Some indefinite pronouns can be singular or plural, including *all, most,* and *some.*

18–40

"<u>All</u> of the people were late for the <u>meeting</u>."

"<u>Most</u> of the time, I feel pretty <u>good</u>."

"<u>Some</u> of the people were <u>upset</u>."

Keep in mind that the main function of a pronoun is to act as a redundant substitute for a noun, and for that reason, it is not emphasized. (Some indefinite pronouns, as above, are exceptions.) A pronoun stands for something, someone, or someplace that has already been introduced, and is therefore part of a continuing discussion about that something, someone, or someplace.

Nouns Treated as Pronouns

Some nouns, by their redundant nature, are treated as pronouns with no emphasis. At the top of this short list is the noun *people*, which is virtually never emphasized.

Here's an example:

18–41

"(People) don't understand the problem with running a <u>city</u>."

"(People) are no damned <u>good</u>."

"That's how it <u>is</u> with (people)."

"If you want (people) to <u>like</u> you, be <u>nice</u> to (people)."

This is also true for the word *Americans*, which can be substituted for *people* in the above examples.

When a pronoun follows a preposition, the *preposition* is emphasized, and the pronoun, as usual, gets no emphasis.

18–42

"Those <u>around</u> (him) admired his <u>courage</u>."

"The problem <u>confounded</u> him for a while, but then he began to <u>understand</u> (it)."

Adjectives and Adverbs

Adjectives and adverbs are *modifiers*; that is, they add a quality to the thing they modify. *Adjectives* describe and clarify the *nouns* and *pronouns* they modify (*pretty, smart, awful, ugly*, etc.).

Adjectives can also point out which one or how many: (every) person, (enough) food, (his) kindness, or (that) store. (Adjectives are in parenthesis.)

Adverbs modify *verbs, adjectives*, or other *adverbs*. They almost always describe when, where, or how: drive (slowly) or (seldom) content. They can also describe other adverbs, as in (too) rapidly.

Some words can act as either adjectives or adverbs, which can create some confusion. You must figure out what word is being described in each situation. Remember that adjectives modify nouns or pronouns only. Adverbs modify verbs, adjectives, and other adverbs.

Consider the modifier *more* in the following examples:

18–43

As an adjective modifying a *noun*: "I want (more) excitement in my life."

As an adverb modifying an *adjective*: "Joan wished she were (more) sophisticated than her friends."

As an adverb modifying an *adverb*. "The (more) rapidly you can accomplish this task, the better."

As an adverb modifying a *verb*: "The boys liked to play (more) than the girls (liked to play)."

One clue to identifying adverbs is to notice that many of them end in *ly*. This does not always identify a word as an adverb, however.

Here is a representative short list of *ly* adverbs:

slowly	enviably	softly	happily
quickly	consummately	mockingly	angrily
passionately	doggedly	carefully	quietly
amicably	hardly	invariably	carefully
effortlessly	congenitally	possibly	mentally
loudly	medically	cordially	fortunately

Here are some exceptions, as *adjectives*:

friendly	wily	dastardly	cowardly

The most important point to remember about adjectives and adverbs is that you must take note of where they appear with respect to the words they modify—whether they *precede* the modified word or *follow* it. This is a very basic rule, so try to remember it: If the modifier precedes the word it modifies, make sure that it does not *overshadow* it. If it follows it, the modifier is *always emphasized*, except in cases of redundancy, which always creates exceptions.

Here are several illustrations.

Preceding Modifier: Adjectives

(Adjectives are in parenthesis; modified nouns are underlined and emphasized.)

18–44

"Alyssa is a very (pretty) girl."

"I had an (exciting) time at the party."

"It's been a long time since we've seen such a (good) movie."

"Terry just bought a (new) car."

"This is an (expensive) cell phone."

Here are examples of adjectives as modifiers that *follow* the modified words:
(Adjectives are underlined and emphasized.)

18–45

"Alyssa is very pretty."

"The party was exciting."

"We haven't seen a movie this good in a long time."

"The car Terry just bought was new."

"This cell phone is expensive."

In the section on "Nouns," read carefully the descriptions and examples of *nouns* acting as modifiers, since nouns as preceding modifiers frequently are treated differently from adjectives.

Many sentences have two or more preceding adjectives in a row.

18–46

"<u>Oliver</u> was a (mean-spirited), (nasty) <u>SOB</u>."

"It was the most (devastating), (depressing), (awful) day of my <u>life</u>."

"He answered her in a (cruel and demeaning) <u>manner</u>."
(Two adjectives are joined by a conjunction.)

Preceding modifiers also appear in groups of two or more, but most of the time, none in the group is emphasized—only the modified noun at the end of the line. There are several examples of this in the chapter on "Destinations."

Also read over the section on "Compound Nouns." Mention is made of compound nouns here because, in a few cases, particularly in medical terms, *adjectives* often function as compound nouns:

18–47

<u>thoracic</u> cavity   <u>religious</u> beliefs
<u>medical</u> records   a <u>dramatic</u> quality
<u>civil</u> disputes

There are several other types of adjectives that you should know.

Possessive Adjectives
(also called *possessive pronouns*)

My, *your*, *his*, *her*, *their*, *our*, and *its*

18–48

"(Her) <u>mother</u> helped her with her <u>home</u>work."

Her is the possessive adjective. It describes whose mother helped her.

Demonstrative Adjectives

That, *those*, *this*, and *these*

18–49

"*Those* people are going to be <u>killed</u> if they don't get out <u>quickly</u>."

In this sentence *those* modifies *people*. We know from this that specific people might be killed.

Interrogative Adjectives

Which and *what*

18–50

"To (what) conversation are you referring?"

"To (which) person were you directing your question?"

Here, *what* modifies *conversation*. It asks what specific conversation is being talked about. The same is the case with *which* modifying *person*.

Indefinite Adjectives

These refer to something identifiable but not specific. Some common indefinite adjectives include *all*, *another*, *something*, *none*, *one*, *several*, and *many*.

18–51

"<u>Several</u> people were absent from the meeting."

In this sentence, *several* is modifying *people*, telling us more about who attended the meeting.

Adjectives generally answer three questions about a noun: How many? What kind? Which ones?

Hot Adjectives

These are adjectives that demand, by their very nature, very animated, emotional emphasis:

18–52

1. "Elaine was <u>astonished</u> when Joe told her Eddie was in jail." (*astonished*)

2. "She was <u>disgusted</u> at the thought of spending the entire evening with Norman." (*disgusted*)

3. "Juan found her to be a <u>captivating beauty</u>." (*captivating*)

4. "The president made a <u>compelling case</u> for removing the banking restrictions." (*compelling*)

Observe that in one and two, the adjective appears after the verb. In three and four, however, the adjective is a preceding modifier, which normally would not be emphasized. Since it is a hot modifier, it is emphasized, and the *noun* is emphasized, since it is the word being modified, consistent with the "don't let a modifier overshadow the word it modifies" rule.

Color Words

In addition to *hot* words in the adjectives previously discussed, there are others that are sometimes referred to as *color* words. Understanding the emotional and psychological implications of these words and the ways to impart this to the listener will greatly enhance your effectiveness as a voice actor.

The most extreme of these color words are those that are *onomatopoeic. Onomatopoeia* refers to a word that vocally sounds like that which it describes. Remember Batman comics? The words *pow*, *bam*, and *zap* are classical examples of onomatopoeia.

Some color words have very crisp attacks at the beginning or the end. Others have a gentle, smooth onset or finish. Long vowels evoke time and distance. Many color words plainly imply the circumstances or activities that they signify.

Consider the following:

18–53

bang	burp	click	crash	caress
cackle	creak	droop	grind	lovely
flutter	crunch	hop	pop	smooth
shoot	fart	rip	tinkle	soft
stretch	giggle	slap	wither	tranquil

Listen to them on the audio track.

Adverbs as Preceding Modifiers

(Adverbs are in parenthesis, and modified words are underlined and emphasized.)

18–54

"Wow, you very (*quickly*) <u>finished</u> that job!" (*quickly* modifies verb *finished*)

"Of all the people in the group with whom my wife could be <u>upset</u>, she was the (most) upset with me." (*most* modifies adjective *upset*)

"The chef (slightly) <u>undercooked</u> the vegetables to preserve their vitamin content." (*slightly* modifies verb *undercooked*)

In all of these examples, there is no emphasis on the adverbs, as they *precede* the words they modify.

Adverbs as Following Modifiers

(Adverbs are italicized and emphasized.)

18–55

"My goodness, you finished that job very *quickly!*"

"Of all the people in the group who were upset with me, my wife was upset the *most.*"

"The chef undercooked the vegetables *slightly,* to preserve the vitamin content."

In these examples, the adverbs are emphasized, as they *follow* the words that they modify.

Prepositions

A *preposition* connects with another word in a sentence, which is either a noun or pronoun. The entire prepositional phrase modifies a word or words that connect with that phrase, and acts as an adjective or adverb.

Typical prepositions include the following:

about	before	despite	like
to	above	behind	down
toward	across	below	during
of	under	after	beneath
except	off	underneath	against
beside	for	on	until
between	from	over	up
among	beyond	in	past
upon	around	by	inside
since	with	at	concerning
into	through	without	throughout

Prepositions can also be placed in one of three categories: *time, place,* and *direction.*

Time prepositions:

after	before	during	since
around	between	for	until
as	by	past	with(in)

Place prepositions:

aboard	above	across	against
around	at	at the back of	at the bottom of
at the top of	between	behind	below
by	in	inside	on the corner of
in the middle of	near	next to	to the left of
to the right of	on	on the side of	on top of
on the other side of	opposite	outside	under(neath)

Direction prepositions:

from	over	through
left	right	under

Common prepositional phrases:

above the clouds	below deck	over the hill
across an ocean	between the lines	since Tuesday
after the fall	by the sea	through the years
against the grain	down the hatch	toward a better future
at 10:00 a.m.	for a month	up the establishment
behind the walls	into the abyss	with the best intentions
beneath the reef	of the people	without a thought

Note that the object is always a *noun* or *pronoun*. Here are prepositional phrases with *pronoun* objects (prepositions are in parenthesis):

18–56

I say, "To <u>hell</u> (with it)."

"This is my <u>gift</u> (for her)."

156

"Mark sensed the danger all <u>around</u> (him)."

The inflection pattern changes in different ways with pronoun objects because pronouns are, by their nature, stand-ins for redundant nouns. In virtually all cases, the pronoun is not emphasized (see "Redundancy and Reiteration"). Note that in some cases, other words may be added between the preposition and its object: articles, adjectives, and adverbs.

18–57

(after) <u>lunch</u>.

(after) a great <u>lunch</u>.

(after) a hastily prepared <u>lunch</u>.

Prepositions are virtually always delivered with a low pitch and a weak beat, like pronouns and conjunctions, as they point to their destination, the object, which gets the emphasis. (See "Destinations.")

Prepositional phrases frequently function as *settings*; that is, they denote *time* and *place*. Here is an example of both time and place in two prepositional phrases. Prepositions are marked in brackets.

18–58

[in] the evening (time) [by] the moonlight (place).

Another example:

"[On] October 12, 1954 (time), just [before] sunup (time), tank and infantry troops [in] the desert (place) prepared [for] <u>battle</u>."

Try not to let a preposition go higher in pitch than the noun that follows it.

Prepositional Phrases Ending with Pronouns

Bearing in mind that since pronouns are redundant by nature, in a prepositional phrase ending with a *pronoun*, the preposition is *emphasized* and the pronoun *de-emphasized*:

18–59

"I wish you'd get <u>with</u> it, pal."

"In spite of his anger at the situation, he knew he had to get <u>over</u> it."

"Are you <u>for</u> me or <u>against</u> me?"

Infinitives

When the preposition *to* is followed by a verb, instead of a noun or pronoun, the combination is called an *infinitive*.

18–60

"I want to help you."

"There is no reason <u>whatsoever</u> (to doubt) his <u>word</u>."

"In spite of his <u>misgivings</u>, he was told not <u>to worry</u>."

The verb in the infinitive can be either transitive or intransitive, and the object can be a noun or pronoun. In the first example, <u>help</u> is emphasized, because the object of the transitive verb, <u>you</u>, is a *pronoun*. In the second example, the verb <u>doubt</u> is not emphasized, because the object of the transitive verb, <u>word</u>, is a *noun*. In the third example, there is no object, since the verb is *intransitive*. Therefore, the emphasis is on the verb <u>worry</u>.

Following are several sentences containing prepositional phrases and infinitives. See if you can identify them. Then practice, record, and play back your delivery:

18–61

1. I always have a glass of wine before dinner.

2. The board faces one of the most difficult tasks in the history of the company.

3. Norman tried to understand her concerns about the upcoming event.

4. In the middle of the night, the Sioux prepared for their attack at dawn.

5. Sarah stood before him, trying to relax within the tense situation.

Although it is considered grammatically improper to end a sentence with a preposition, it has become common practice in conversation. Hence, you may occasionally encounter it in voice over scripts.

18–62

Conversational (Informal)	Formal
"Which team are you rooting for?"	"For which team are you rooting?"
"What tools are you working with?"	"With what tools are you working?"
"Whom are you partial to?"	"To whom are you partial?"

Many prepositions can also be used as adverbs.

Here are examples of prepositions used as adverbs:

"I saw the truck pass <u>by</u>."

"The midshipmen <u>below</u> were killed or injured."

Here are more examples of prepositions:

"I saw the <u>truck</u> pass (by) my <u>house</u>."

"The midshipmen (below) <u>deck</u> were killed or <u>injured</u>."

Prepositions can also exist as more than one word. Here are several:

according to	as early as	ahead of
because of	as late as	as to
close to	as much as	up to
ahead of	in between	in view of
aside from	in spite of	on top of

thanks to	similar to	at the expense of
except for	in place of	by the time of
along with	in keeping with	at the mercy of
prior to	with respect to	by way of

EXERCISES

Identify the prepositions; then identify and underline objects. Then practice, record, and play back your delivery:

1. According to a recent survey, math scores in the United States are behind most of the other developed countries'.

   Without ambition and a desire to persist, true success is unlikely for many college students today.

2. When archaeologists went inside the tomb, they discovered several mummified bodies, in keeping with their theory that the tomb was built for only a pharaoh.

3. The Senate made a difficult decision at the expense of the poorer people of many American cities, in spite of an improving economy.

4. Edward rose to the top of his class, ahead of his nearest rivals, thanks to the help of influential people with whom he was connected, in keeping with his manipulating ways.

5. In view of citizen dissatisfaction with the status quo, the mayor felt that he must act quickly or face impeachment as early as the following Monday after Labor Day.

Remember that prepositions always lead to a destination—the *object*.

Conjunctions

Conjunctions are linguistic connective tissue. They connect words, phrases, or clauses. They also lead into the last entity in a *list*. The most common conjunctions are *and, or, if, but, when,* and *as*. Conjunctions should not be emphasized, as they are only connectors. In hard- or medium-sell radio or television commercials, the use of an emphasized *and* or *or* has become a favorite gimmick of some ad-agency producers. Emphasizing conjunctions has also worked its way into local TV newscasters' bags of tricks. In all other situations, and especially in narration work, they are always de-emphasized.

Here are some examples of conjunctions as described in the first paragraph:

Connecting *words*:

18–63

apples and <u>oranges</u>	red or <u>green</u>
beautiful but <u>stupid</u>	polite if <u>formal</u>
slippery when <u>wet</u>	ruler as <u>politician</u>

Connecting *phrases*:

18–64

"Before you <u>leave</u> (or) when I <u>return</u>."

"Leave the file on the <u>desk</u> (or) in the <u>drawer</u>."

"Are you for me (or) <u>against</u> me?"

"(Both) people who work for <u>themselves</u> (and) those who work for <u>companies</u> will <u>vote</u> for the proposal."

Connecting *clauses*:

18–65

"I enjoyed the <u>show</u>, (but) I was disappointed with the main <u>character</u>."

(two independent clauses)

The children played <u>outside</u> for over two <u>hours,</u> (as) they were tired of being <u>inside</u> for days due to the unrelenting <u>snowstorms</u>." (independent/dependent clauses)

"He married her in <u>spite</u> of his parents' objections (but) realizing a year <u>later</u> he had made a big <u>mistake</u>." (two independent clauses)

*Remember to always *pause* before the conjunction. Never rush a clause into a conjunction without pausing, unless you're describing two single entities connected by a conjunction.

There are three categories of conjunctions: *coordinating,* *subordinating,* and *correlative. Coordinating conjunctions* connect sentence elements of the same grammatical classification (nouns with nouns, adjectives with adjectives, etc.).

Coordinating conjunctions are limited to the following: *and, but, or, nor, for, yet,* and *so.*

18–66

"The peasants could only fight with pikes (and) <u>rifles</u>." (nouns)

"My friends would always praise (or) <u>criticize</u> me." (verbs)

"Slowly (but) intensely, the noise increased." (adverbs)

"The children ran around corners (and) through the <u>house</u>." (two prepositional phrases)

"The team almost never <u>won,</u> (but) they wouldn't give <u>up</u>."(clauses)

"I had good <u>instincts</u> about her, (so) I asked her <u>out</u>." (clauses)

Subordinate conjunctions connect subordinate clauses to a sentence element in a main clause.

Some examples include the following: *after, because, if, that, though, unless, until, when,* and *whether.*

Adverb clauses (used as adverbs):

18–67

"I'm not <u>coming</u>, (because) I am <u>ill</u>."

"(Before) you get <u>upset</u>, listen to what I have to say." (Here the adverb clause *precedes* the main clause. It has been turned around.)

"We will fail the <u>course</u> (if) we don't study for the <u>exam</u>."

"You children will catch a <u>cold</u> (unless) you come into the house <u>now</u>."

Noun clauses (used as nouns):

18–68

"Mary believes (that) <u>no</u> one <u>likes</u> her."

"Do you know (where) the wine cellar is?"

"I need to know (whether) this coin is <u>worth</u> anything."

"They need to know (how) we can <u>accomplish</u> this."

Correlative conjunctions are always used in pairs.

Some examples:

both/and either/or

not only/but neither/nor

The following are examples of coordination in sentences:

18–69

"This proposal will appeal to both men and <u>women</u>."

"You are (not only) mean-<u>spirited</u> (but) <u>vengeful</u>."

"She is (neither) pretty (nor) <u>nice</u>."

"(Either) you drop that <u>gun</u>, (or) I <u>shoot</u>."

Note that when two entities are joined by a conjunction, the one that *follows* the conjunction gets the emphasis, unless, for dramatic purposes, the preceding entity calls for emphasis as well. However, the stronger emphasis will still be on the one that follows the conjunction.

Finally, conjunctions are also used to lead into the last entity in a list. Remember that entities in a list can be single words, phrases, or clauses. (See "Lists.")

18–70

Single words:

"Apples, pears, oranges, pineapples, (and) <u>bananas</u>."

Two words:

"Pretty <u>girls</u>, handsome <u>men</u>, (and) wonderful <u>evenings</u> together."

Phrases:

"Over the <u>river</u>, through the <u>woods</u>, down the <u>streets</u>, and into the mall."

Clauses:

"I got in my <u>car</u>, drove to the <u>airport</u>, picked up my <u>girlfriend</u>, (and) brought her <u>home</u> with me."

As with prepositions and pronouns, the conjunction is delivered as a low-note, weak-beat word. No emphasis. Remember, it's only a *connector*.

This is a chapter that should be revisited often until it is mastered. If you are able to recognize and identify parts of speech and understand how they interact, the quality and effectiveness of your reads will improve immeasurably, especially on narrations and audiobooks.

Just for Fun

She looked over at the natty noun, who was brazenly dangling his participle at her, while looking over her modifiers. He made an outrageous preposition to her. Ignoring his effusive verbalizing, she connected with a massive conjunction, hitting him so hard, she split his infinitive. At this juncture, he concluded that she could no longer be the object of his inflections.

Quick Grammar Review

Only in grammar can you be more than perfect.

—William Safire (1929–2009), Author

PARTS OF SPEECH

Nouns

Subjects, objects, *pictures*—person, place, or thing. The most image-evoking parts of speech in any script.

Verbs

Actions, activities—moving dynamics—contribute more than any other part of speech to the real drama.

Transitive verb: acts on a direct object; in this situation, go through the verb and highlight the direct object. If it takes a pronoun object, highlight the verb.

Intransitive verb: has no object; it is its own action. Therefore, the verb itself is highlighted.

Adjectives

Modify, describe, qualify, and quantify nouns. When they precede nouns, they must never overshadow them; when alone at the end of a phrase or clause, they are always emphasized.

Some examples of preceding adjectives: (pretty) girl, (slow) speed, (happy) camper, (heavy) hitter, (awful) mess, (sour) grapes, (clever) idea

Adverbs

Modify, describe, and qualify verbs, adjectives, and other adverbs.

165

When they precede the word they modify, the same rule applies as with adjectives, as well as when alone.

Some examples of preceding adverbs: (so) menacing, (just) happened, (ever) watchful, (even) more

Conjunctions

Connectors—two single entities (*yours and mine*), the end of a list (*apples, pears, and oranges*), bridging an independent clause with a dependent clause or bridging between two independent clauses.

Approach conjunctions with a low-note, weak-beat feel.

Examples: *and, but, or, if, as, when*

Prepositions

Direction, position, lead-in to settings (time and place)

Same approach as with conjunctions: low note, weak beat

Examples: *of, about, for, between, among, under, over, around, in, out, with, within, without, by*

Pronouns

second-time introduction of a previously stated noun, either by actuality or implication

Examples: *I, we, us, you, he, she, her, him, they, them, it, one*

Don't overlook *possessive* pronouns: *my, our, your, his, her, their.*

Chapter Nineteen

COMPOUND NOUNS AND SIMILAR COMBINATIONS

You can recognize a well-tuned phrase or an elegant style. But when you are applying the rules of grammar skillfully, you ascend to another level of the beauty of language.

—Muriel Barbery (1969–present), Author

B ecause so many of my students have been confounded by the material that follows, as have over 80 percent of all local and national newscasters in the media and a significant number of working voice over actors, I am giving this material a chapter of its own.

In addition to serving as subjects and objects, *nouns* can also be used as *adjectives*. In most of these cases, instead of having little or no emphasis as a preceding modifier, since it is a noun, it will get the emphasis, and the second noun it modifies will not. Noun combinations used in this way are called *compound nouns*.

Some examples:

19–1

Brain power, aircraft parts, landing gear, propeller shaft, landfill operator, music hall, flower grower, jockey shorts, garter belt, power generator

167

Medical terms:

19–2

> Blood test, beta blocker, cell count, femoral artery, food poisoning, heat exhaustion, immune system, jugular vein, life cycle, mood disorder, oxygen mask, pituitary gland, root canal, test tube

Medical terms associated with the name of the person who was the discoverer or a victim of the disease, for whom the disease is now named: (the discoverer's name is used as an *adjective* but still gets the emphasis).

> Crohn's disease, Cushing's syndrome, Alzheimer's disease, Lou Gehrig's disease

Here are some exceptions to first-word emphasis, where both modifier and modified are nouns:

19–3

> Black Death, balloon catheter, group practice, root cause, inferiority complex, pituitary tumor

Most medical and chemical compounds, however, treat the preceding noun modifier as an adjective.

19–4

> Ethylene glycol, ammonium nitrate, sulfuric acid, potassium chloride, gamma globulin, sodium carbonate, bismuth subnitrate, nitrous oxide

Here is the compound noun applied to *technical terms*:

9–5

> Machine shop, die cutter, band saw, metal lathe, blow torch, power washer

And here is the application to *construction equipment*:

19–6

Concrete crusher, pile driver, steam shovel, dump truck, backhoe (one word from two), and bulldozer (one word from two)

to *camera gear*:

19–7

lens hood, iris control, viewfinder (one word from two), camera body, flash gun.

to *audio/video* gear:

19–8

CD recorder, video recorder, edit controller, microphone stand, speaker system, volume control, power amplifier, jukebox (one word from two) (exception: video monitor)

to *computer gear*:

19–9

Computer screen, keyboard (one word from two), USB connector, screen display, FireWire (one word from two), workstation (one word from two) (exceptions: computer interface, computer software)

Here is a series of combinations involving the word *animal* as the first noun. The left column illustrates the emphasis on the first word as a *noun* modifier. The right column illustrates the use of the first noun used and treated as a normal preceding *adjective* modifier, with the emphasis placed on the second word:

19–10

animal control	animal husbandry
animal crackers	animal instincts
animal films	animal science
Animal Planet	animal communication

Now here is a series of combinations involving not nouns but *adjectives* and nouns ending in *ic* and *il*, with the emphasis in each column as in the above examples:

19–11

<u>civic</u> religion	civic <u>responsibility</u>
<u>gastric</u> juices	gastric <u>bypass</u>
<u>rheumatic</u> diseases	rheumatic <u>fever</u>
<u>civil</u> disputes	Civil <u>War</u>

You have probably come to the correct conclusion by now that many of these combinations need to be learned as *vocabulary*, since there are so many exceptions to the usual noun combinations. Note also that there exist combinations of three or more nouns in a row—in effect, one combination wrapped inside another.

19–12

<u>bean</u>bag chair, <u>income</u> tax rate, <u>stock</u>-market conditions, <u>credit</u>-card companies, <u>trash</u>-can fires, <u>test</u>-tube baby, <u>immune</u> deficiency syndrome, <u>blood</u>-donor services, <u>gun</u>-control advocate, <u>labor</u>-saving devices.

Now here's an example with an adjective as the first word: battered-<u>child</u> syndrome.

19–13

Three nouns in combination, but the first and second have become a combined word: <u>bed</u>side manner.

19–14

Here's a three-word combination with two adjectives instead of nouns, but the first functions as a normal preceding modifier, while the second performs as the nouns illustrated earlier: obsessive-<u>compulsive</u> disorder.

Now here are three-noun combinations, in which the first two act as preceding adjectives, and the emphasis falls on the last noun. This is a strong exception to everything illustrated so far.

19–15

Peanut-butter <u>sandwich</u> (not <u>peanut</u> butter sandwich, or peanut <u>butter</u> sandwich).

Now let's consider the possible variations in emphasis progressively created by extended *destinations* (see "Destinations"), built around the noun combination *milk shake*:

19–16

<u>milk</u> shake, Chicago <u>milk</u> shake, Chicago-<u>milk</u>-shake machine, Chicago-<u>milk</u>-shake-machine salesman.

Now here's the same line operating as a long descriptive *title*:

19–17

"Chicago-milk-shake-machine-salesman Ray <u>Murphy</u>."

Remember that since this is a long title in front of a proper name, only the surname *Murphy* gets the emphasis.

Here's an example of a compound noun as a *destination* extended by add-on modifiers:

19–18

"Wake Forest <u>research</u> team."
"Wake Forest University <u>research</u> team."
"Wake Forest University Baptist <u>research</u> team."
"Wake Forest University Baptist medical-<u>research</u> team."
"Wake Forest University Baptist Medical Center <u>research</u> team."

As you can see, the modifiers can add up; therefore, you need to look ahead carefully to discern the final destination, the compound noun *research team*.

Regarding technical and medical terminology, no producer or director expects you to come to the table knowing even a high percentage of industry-specific and medical/technical vocabulary. However, the more exposure you have to these words and combinations of words, the better, as it will give you an upper hand in your comprehension of those particular areas of the voice over art.

Even the last of a group of initials standing for the name of an organization or other entity can function as a compound noun:

19–19

"I'm an AOP<u>A</u> member."

"AS<u>A</u> rules prohibit political interference."

"He needs to see a doctor who understands ST<u>D</u> symptoms."

Think of a compound noun combination as forming a *single word*, with the strong syllable in the first word and the remaining syllables all with no emphasis. Don't pause in between the words in combination, or you will be unconsciously compelled to emphasize the second word (the one being modified). Remember that if the combination were *coordinating*, the emphasis would be on the second word, and the first word, the modifier, would get *no* emphasis. Remember that the definite characteristic of a compound noun is that the *modifier* gets the emphasis, not the word it modifies.

Chapter Twenty

In-Depth Guide to Emphasis and De-Emphasis

This chapter reviews and further demonstrates several concepts that were previously introduced, adds new concepts, and finally, focuses on specific words and word combinations that appear frequently in voiceover scripts.

Words to Emphasize

Nouns (new nouns that are introduced for the first time)

<u>20–1</u>

"The <u>lion</u> eats his <u>prey</u> under the <u>tree</u>."

(The verb *eats* is *transitive*. The action goes through, or across, the verb, hence the prefix *trans*, and acts on the object, making it dramatically the strongest noun in the sentence.)

Subject: *lion*

Object of verb: *prey*

Object of preposition: *tree*

Note that these principles apply only to nouns that are introduced for the *first time*; that is, they are not already introduced as part of the story. (See "Redundancy and Reiteration.")

20–2

"John F. Kennedy was a man of many contradictions."

"The Gold Rush of 1849 captivated many who dreamed of great riches."

Nouns that are objects of *transitive verbs*

"In spite of his best efforts, he failed the test."

"For the first time in my life, I bought a Mercedes."

Nouns that are objects of *prepositions*

"On a bitter, cold, and windy day, many people contracted respiratory illnesses."

"By morning, the crisis had come to a head."

Exclamations

20–3

"Unbelievable! They won by seventeen points!"

"Gosh! I had no idea they came from my hometown!"

Hot Transitive Verbs

20–4

"The adulation of millions of fans catapulted performers to an almost worshipped status."

"The stories of successful emigrants colonized the imaginations of many ordinary Americans."

Intransitive Verbs

20–5

"When asked what she wanted to do with her life, she answered, 'I just want to dance.'"

THE VOICE OVER ACTOR'S HANDBOOK

"As a primary manifestation of her dysfunction, Alice <u>pouted</u> frequently."

Transitive Verbs That Act on Pronoun Objects
<u>20–6</u>

"Stravinsky <u>composed</u> (himself) before being introduced as the keynote speaker at the symposium."

"The members of the Board <u>assured</u> (themselves) that they had made the right decision."

Transitional Adverbs
<u>20–7</u>

"<u>Initially</u>, his work was thorough. <u>Later on</u>, it reflected his lack of preparation."

"He was impressed with the design of the building. <u>Moreover</u>, the landscaping reminded him of a French estate he had once visited."

Hot Words

Occasionally, an adjective or adverb is used for dramatic emphasis. These might be referred to as "hot" modifiers. They should be emphasized with vigor, as opposed to low-drama, or "cool," modifiers.

Here are some examples. The second and fourth are preceded by a sentence that uses a low-drama, or cool, modifier.

<u>20-8</u>

Adjective:
"Barbara was a (real) <u>beauty</u>." (cool)
"Barbara was a <u>stunning beauty</u>." (hot)

Adverb:
"Barbara was (really) <u>beautiful</u>." (cool)
"Barbara was <u>stunningly beautiful</u>." (hot)

Onomatopoeia

The most extreme of the hot words are those that are *onomatopoetic*. *Onomatopoeia* refers to a word that vocally replicates a sound or action. Remember Batman comics? *Crraack*, *Krunch*, *Sploosh*, and *Whack* are classic examples of onomatopoeia.

Color Words

In addition to *hot* words previously discussed, there are other modifiers that are sometimes referred to as *color* words. Understanding the emotional and psychological implications of these words and the ways to impart this to the listener will greatly enhance your effectiveness.

Some hot or color words have very crisp attacks at the beginning or the end. Others have a gentle, smooth onset or finish. Long vowels evoke time and distance. Many color words plainly imply the circumstance or activity they signify.

Consider the following:

20-9

Onomatopoeia:			Color Adjectives:	
muffle	guffaw	snap	mushy	blistering
gurgle	glug	crackle	moody	sizzling
whirr	groan	pop	velvety	sticky
hiccup	growl	honk	dulcet	fiery
meow	moan	slurp	rapturous	hot
bark	hoot	click	quiet	torrid
flip-flop	hum	droop	pleasant	steamy

Transitional Adverbs

Transitional adverbs are most often used at beginnings of sentences. They are referred to as transitional because they create a transitional space between what came before them and what follows them.

Examples are *yesterday, today, tomorrow, moreover, however,* and *finally.*

20-10

"Yesterday, Jack felt as if his world were closing in on him. Today, after getting a good night's sleep, he feels much better and more positive about his life. Tomorrow, he should be back to normal."

Note that *yesterday, today,* and *tomorrow* are also one-word *settings.*

"The outlook for the company over the next ten years is very optimistic. However, there are potential obstacles along the way."

Ends of Sentences

All sentences should end in a strong declarative (statement) emphasis, almost always on the last word in the sentence, except for colloquial sentences, passive voice, and throwaway prepositional phrases acting as settings.

20-11

"This machine is made exclusively for one purpose."

"That man is a real curmudgeon."

"It was an event that surpassed many great moments in history."

"He was the architect of the total reorganization of Britain's army."

Nouns in a Stream-of-Consciousness Series

Occasionally, a line will be written in a string of nouns, with each attaching a further meaning to the first noun, in one stream of consciousness after another. Each noun will be emphasized as a statement and progressively emphasized with more emotional intensity.

20-12

"They were friends, comrades, lovers."

Compound Nouns

A compound noun, in most situations, involves a noun modifying another noun. A normal adjective simply flows into the noun that follows and is modified by it.

20–13

"Dr. Bretton is a good <u>surgeon</u>."

(*good* is not emphasized; hence the term *coordinate*)

"Dr. Bretton is a <u>brain</u> surgeon."

(*brain* is now emphasized, not surgeon; hence the term *compound noun*)

Some types of adjectives are used as part of a compound noun. These include many adjectives ending in *al*: <u>medical</u> records, <u>legal</u> terms, but not animal <u>husbandry</u>, a normal <u>reaction</u>, for example. There are many exceptions of *al* adjectives, as well as other suffixes, which often must be learned as new vocabulary words:

<u>civil</u> disputes (compound noun)
Civil <u>War</u> (adjective modifies noun)
civil <u>unrest</u> (adjective modifies noun)

There are also situations where one compound noun is paired with another:

"Kathmandu is a <u>tourist</u> and <u>mountain</u>-climbing mecca."
(*Tourist* mecca is the first; *mountain*-climbing mecca is the second. Note that *mountain* climbing is also a compound noun by itself.)

Adjectives in a Stream of Consciousness Series

The same treatment applies to *adjectives* in a series.

20-14

"Many found the king to be <u>tolerant</u>, <u>broadminded</u>, <u>brilliant</u>, and intensely <u>moral</u>. Others found him <u>hypocritical</u>, <u>devious</u>, <u>philistine</u>, <u>cruel</u>."

178

One-Word Settings

20–15

"Today, the infrastructure of the country is in dire need of serious improvement."

"Years ago, people scoffed at the idea of nonelected superdelegates. Now, they're in disbelief at the present state of election customs."

Demonstrative Pronouns

20–16

"This is where I always wanted to be."

"Those are the school bullies I told you about."

Comparison/Contrast

20–17

"Are you for me or against me?"

"Whose side are you on, his or mine?"

"Jenny likes apples. Susie prefers oranges." (Double comparison)

As you can see, this principle applies to various parts of speech.

The Last Item in a List

20–18

"Apples, pears, oranges, pineapples and bananas."

"My grandfather was a cantankerous, crotchety, feisty old man."

"As was usual for him, he was misinterpreted, misunderstood, misrepresented."

"(Elephant) ears, (crossed) eyes, (two) noses."

"He was a good father, a considerate husband, and a fine human being."

"They believed in their <u>faith</u>, their indomitable <u>will</u>, their <u>persistence</u>, and their hard <u>work</u>."

Comparing/Contrasting Words

These include *other*, *others*, and *another*.

Look for a comparing or contrasting event when using one of these three words. In almost all cases, the noun that follows *other* or *another* is not emphasized, because it is *redundant* (see "Redundancy and Reiteration").

20–19

"Most medicines are safe; <u>other</u> (medicines) carry a great risk of side effects."

"Some said it couldn't be done. <u>Others</u> were more optimistic."

Others is a comparing entity by itself. It is not a modifier. *Another* can be used either way.

As a modifier:

"One evening we went to a show. On <u>another</u> (evening), we had a fabulous dinner."

As a single comparing entity:

"Two of the visitors rode with us. <u>Another</u> rode with my brother and his wife."

Here's an example of *another* modifying a *nonredundant noun*, where it is *not* emphasized:

"The relaxation of the rules of disclosure was (another) financial <u>bonanza</u> for Wall Street."

Also

Also is used as an add-on to indicate a second event like the first or a different event added on.

20–20

(Same event)	"Norma flunked the test yesterday. Several other students <u>also</u> flunked it."
(Add-on event)	"Making movies was very time consuming and a lot of work. It was <u>also</u>, as Orson Welles said, 'The biggest toy train set any boy ever had.'"

In both examples, we emphasize and animate *also*, to make a strong point.

Conjunctions connecting *individual entities*:

20–21

The first entity is almost never emphasized. The second is always emphasized and always more than the first.

"Fine (and) <u>dandy</u>. Beautiful (but) <u>stupid</u>. The beginning (or) the <u>end</u>."

Sometimes, for dramatic effect, the *first* word is emphasized. However, the *second* word, as stated before, still gets the stronger emphasis:

"He was <u>stunned</u> (and) <u>surprised</u> by the man's reply to his question."

Conjunctions connecting to the last item in a *list*:

As you approach the last item, pause before the conjunction and put the strongest emphasis on the last item, and let the conjunction flow into it.

20–22

As a true connected list, delivered without inflecting each item:

"Apples, pears, oranges, pineapples, and <u>bananas</u>." (emphasis only on *bananas*)

Or, deliver with an inflection on each item:

"Apples, pears, oranges, pineapples, (animate *pineapples* with an anticipatory inflection followed by a pause) and bananas."
(strongest emphasis on *bananas*)

Parts of Speech That Are Almost Never Emphasized

Redundant Words

If a noun is repeated in the context of a continually developing story or treatment (sometimes several times), that noun is not emphasized, because it is already well-established. People unconsciously keep track of these nouns (and other pertinent parts of speech) as they talk through a subject in ordinary conversation and in presentations. In the examples, de-emphasized words are in parenthesis.

Note also that almost all words that are de-emphasized should be pitched as comfortably low as possible.

20-23

"The men boarded the submarine. They had no idea that within days, the (submarine) would be sunk, and they would not come back alive."

"He loved Marianne. (Marianne) loved him even more."

"Thomas Jefferson was one of our greatest presidents. Many aspects of slavery bothered (Jefferson), and he tried to give some degree of freedom to his (slaves)."

Remember also that this applies to synonymous words, or even phrases that replace the already established word, phrase, or sentence.

20-24

"As soon as the family was able to travel, they boarded their van and set off for Seattle. It was a long and arduous (journey), as they were inexperienced travelers."

(Here, *journey* is de-emphasized, as it is a word that stands for the act of traveling, as described in the first sentence with the words *travel* and *set off*, and is therefore redundant.)

"He was able to work at his own <u>pace</u> and establish his own <u>deadlines</u>, at a time when others did not <u>enjoy</u> (those luxuries)."

(*Those luxuries* is de-emphasized because it stands for the privileges stated in the first two clauses.)

The exception to this de-emphasis is in <u>reiteration</u>, where the repeating of the word is done for special emphasis.

"We'll <u>double</u> the repair period of the manufacturer's warranty. <u>Double</u> it, or your money back!"

Redundant words, mostly nouns and verbs, don't need emphasis.

Redundant words are in parenthesis:

20–25

"This is <u>Adele</u>, the (woman) I told you about."

"The battle began at dawn. By day's end, the soldiers were so <u>exhausted</u> (from the battle), they could no longer fight <u>on</u>."

Reminder: The exception to these no-emphasis scenarios is *reiteration*, where the repeating of the word in question is emphasized for dramatic effect.

"You are not to come here again. I repeat. You are <u>not</u> to come here again."

Pronouns

The pronoun is by definition a stand-in for a redundant noun, either as a follow-up to a noun in the third person (he, she, they, it, one) or by implication, as in the first (I, me, we) and the second person (you).

183

20–26

First/second person: "(You) know what (I) mean, <u>don't</u> (you)?"

The *I* and *you* are the persons already in each other's presence, and on whose mutual communication an implicit assumption of redundancy is made, based on that presence.

There is an exception:

Never address your listener with an emphasized *you* unless you are comparing or contrasting him or her with someone else.

20–27

"If <u>you</u> can do it, <u>I</u> can do it." (comparison)

"Maybe <u>you</u> can do it, but <u>I</u> can't." (contrast)

Here's another example of redundancy, using the first and third person:

"(I) ran into Mary in the drugstore, and (she) told me about her problems with her boss."

Note also that the *possessive* pronoun *her* is used twice in this sentence.

Prepositions

Prepositions denote position or direction. They always lead to a *noun* (or *pronoun*, with a redundant noun implied by the pronoun). Treat the preposition as a low note on a weak beat, and build as you approach the noun at the end of the phrase.

20–28

"(Under) a <u>tree</u>. (Around) the <u>corner</u>. (Over) the river and (through) the woods (to) Grandmother's house we go."

However, if the preposition leads into a *pronoun*, emphasize the *preposition*, not the pronoun—just the *reverse* of the preposition-to-noun phrase.

20–29

"Although it had been 3 years since he had been with Amy, he knew he still <u>loved</u> (her)."

"In spite of careful aiming at the target, he <u>missed</u> (it)."

Conjunctions

Conjunctions are connective tissue. Consider the root of the word: they *conjoin* words, phrases, clauses, and ends of lists. As with prepositions, treat them as weak beats leading into phrases or clauses that follow them.

20–30

"I wanted to see her (and) renew our friendship, (but) I wasn't sure (if) she wanted to see me. Then I decided to chance it (and) approach her."

"I went to the show (and) liked it a lot (but) wasn't sure if I should have (or) not. Then I waited (and) read the review, (so) I could relax (and) discuss it with you."

Transitive Verbs with Pronoun Objects

The pronoun object is a stand-in for a noun that has been previously introduced into the script; in the case of the following examples, the noun is introduced in the same sentence:

20–31

"I <u>love</u> (you), Alice."

"I cannot <u>help</u> (you)."

"Tony really <u>nailed</u> (it) when he referred to the man's poor record in office."

"I <u>composed</u> (myself) before getting up to deliver my speech."

"After months of reports of Jim's shoddy work, the company finally <u>fired</u> (him)."

First/Middle Names and Titles Preceding Proper Names

Remember to emphasize only the *surname* in a proper name, with or without a title.

20-32

(John) <u>Whittier</u>

(John Greenleaf) <u>Whittier</u>

(George Herbert Walker) <u>Bush</u>

(President George H. W.) <u>Bush</u>

(King George the) <u>Fifth</u>

Beginnings of Most Sentences

Most sentences should begin with a low note and weak beat, unless they start with an exclamation, such as *wow!* or a demonstrative pronoun, such as *this/these*.

20-33

"(There) are new forces at work in this industry."

"(It) has no equal in the world."

"(Be) it endless fascination with magic."

"(Uncover) the truth behind the mystery."

Endings of Colloquial Sentences

Colloquial sentences are informal expressions that have worked their way into the language. They always end in a throwaway inflection.

20-34

"My wife <u>works</u> (too hard)."

"Our <u>survival</u> (is at stake)."

"The <u>boss</u> (wants to see you)."

Preceding Modifiers
(adjectives and adverbs)

Adjectives modify *nouns*. Adverbs modify *verbs*, *adjectives*, and *other adverbs*.

Never let a preceding modifier overshadow the word it modifies.

20–35

"A (pretty) <u>girl</u> is like a <u>melody</u>."
(*pretty* is an adjective, modifying the noun *girl*)

"Adam did (very) <u>well</u> on the <u>test</u>."
(*very* is an adverb modifying the adverb *well*)

"<u>Today</u> was (mostly) <u>sunny</u>."
(*mostly* is an adverb modifying the adjective *sunny*)

"It was <u>years</u> before he (first) <u>allowed</u> (himself) the freedom he <u>needed</u>." (*first* is an adverb modifying the verb *allowed*)

Auxiliary Verbs

These include *should, could, would, might*, etc.

Auxiliary verbs complement a main verb and should always be secondary to it. Therefore, they should not be emphasized.

20–36

"Your <u>father</u> (should) understand how you <u>feel</u> about this."
(*Should* flows right through the sentence and is not emphasized.)

"I might have <u>helped</u> him, had he asked."

(*Might* flows through, as in the previous example.)

Compound Modifiers

Again, follow the rule for preceding modifiers. The only difference here is that there is more than one modifier:

20–37

"They serviced the working and damaged <u>motors</u>."

"There are creative and stimulating <u>drives</u> at work in this industry."

Rarely, there will be emphasis on the second modifier if it is a *hot* modifier:

"She gave a moving and <u>brilliant</u> <u>performance</u>."

"The car gives you a taut, yet <u>silken</u> <u>ride</u>."

Remember not to let the emphasis on the second modifier overshadow the noun it modifies, according to the rule on preceding modifiers.

A Preposition That Extends the Destination of a Phrase

The emphasis moves from the preceding word to the end of the prepositional phrase. It weakens the word that precedes it.

20–38

"We offer clients with created or inherited <u>wealth</u> a full set of complimentary services."

Clients is de-emphasized by "with created or inherited <u>wealth</u>." *Wealth* is now the point of emphasis.

"Many citizens are on a quest for a healthy <u>environment</u>."

Quest is de-emphasized in favor of *environment*.

Modifiers That Extend Destinations

20–39

Example: "His mother was the most (conniving), (controlling), (manipulative) woman I ever <u>observed</u>."

Any Word or Combination of Words That Extend a Destination

20–40

"It was the most (massive), (expensive), (single effort) (ever) <u>attempted</u>."

(The combination of adjectives *massive*, *expensive*, and *single*, the noun *effort*, and the adverb *ever* are de-emphasized, in favor of the destination *attempted*.)

Remember also that *prepositional phrases* extend destinations.

Not, never, ever, even, either/or, or neither/nor

20–41

"I will (not) <u>help</u> you with your homework."

"He (never) <u>impressed</u> me much."

"Don't (ever) do <u>that</u> again," or "Don't (ever) do that <u>again</u>."

"She (even) had the nerve to ask me something <u>personal</u>."

"(Either) you tell her the truth about what <u>happened</u> (or) I will."

"(Neither) Samantha (nor) her <u>husband</u> remembered <u>meeting</u> me last year."

Other words that extend destinations include *that, which, who, whom, where, why,* and *how.*

20–42

"He is definitely a man (who) <u>talks</u> too much."

189

"She is the woman about (whom) I told you."

(same as "(whom) I told you about")

"It is a place (where) evenings are filled with entertainment."

"Choose the one that suits you <u>best</u>."

(If it were only "suits you," the emphasis would be on *suits*. *Which* can also be used.)

"My teacher has no idea (how) to do this problem."

"I don't know (why) I love her."

Bear in mind that in today's usage, the word *that* may also be *implied*.

20–43

Written as:

"I don't (believe) they've spent a day apart since their wedding day."

Same as:

"I don't (believe that) they've spent a day apart since their wedding day."

Other words that are almost never emphasized:

As...as

This is always a connecting phrase, with no emphasis within it.

20–44

"This is (as close as) you can <u>get</u> to finding your joy."

"I like <u>popcorn</u> almost (as much as) I like <u>peanut butter</u>."

"She is not (as compromising as) I once <u>believed</u> she was."

"(As long as) you stay out of my <u>way</u>, we won't have any <u>problems</u>."

Either...or, neither...nor

These always *lead into* the words that follow them.

190

20–45

"(Either) you give us your <u>gun</u>, (or) we'll <u>shoot</u>."

"(Neither) a borrower (nor) a <u>lender be</u>."

Never

This is almost always de-emphasized, except in very strong dramatic situations; it's a *preceding modifier*:

20–46

"I will (never) speak to you <u>again</u>."

"(Never) in all my <u>life</u> have I heard such <u>drivel</u> from an otherwise intelligent <u>man</u>."

Enough

This is treated as an adverb when placed *after* the word it modifies.

20–47

"My cold is not <u>severe</u> (enough) to keep me inside."

"Even with a sweater on, he was not <u>warm</u> (enough)."

So

This is an adverb that is never emphasized when ahead of the word it modifies.

20–48

"Why did he become (so) <u>popular</u> (so) <u>quickly</u>?"

"There are (so) many <u>people</u> involved in this disaster that we will never know who is truly responsible."

Not

This is a simple adverb that makes a negative out of a positive, and it's a preceding modifier, as with *never*.

20–49

"Do (not) try to <u>stop</u> me from speaking my <u>mind</u>."

"You are (not) my <u>friend</u> any <u>longer</u>."

Than

Than can function as a preposition or a conjunction.

20–50

(As a preposition)	"I'm a lot smarter (than) you."
(As a conjunction)	"The meeting took much longer (than) he had planned."
(As a conjunction with *other*)	"(Other than) my wife, I can't think of anyone I trust completely."

People

People is almost never emphasized because it is by its very nature redundant. People are everywhere at once.

20–51

"(People) are always <u>bothering</u> me."

"So many (people) are <u>rude</u> these days."

Americans

We don't emphasize *Americans* for the same reason we don't emphasize *people*. Americans are already *in* America.

20–52

"(Americans) are very upset with Congress and the Supreme Court."

"In this country, it is difficult for many political <u>candidates</u> to connect with a <u>majority</u> (of Americans.)

Going to...

Never emphasize *going* when followed by a *to* that is followed by a *verb*, making it an *infinitive*.

20–53

"I could tell <u>immediately</u> that they were not (going to) <u>help</u> us."

"Alan was told that the school was going to <u>restrict</u> his off-campus <u>privileges</u>."

Words Preceding Infinitives

These words can be *nouns* or *verbs*.

20–54

"It was a beautiful, sunny day. There was no (need) to shield the president's open convertible from inclement weather." (*noun* precedes infinitive)

"He ran toward the shore, jumped into the water, and (tried) to save the young child." (*verb* precedes infinitive)

Modifiers That Extend Destinations

20–55

"He was the (angriest), (nastiest), (most mean-spirited) man I ever <u>met</u>." (adjectives)

Any Word or Combination of Words That Extend a Destination

"It was the most (massive), (expensive), (single effort) (ever) attempted."

(The combination of adjectives *massive*, *expensive*, and *single*, the noun *effort*, and the adverb *ever* are de-emphasized, in favor of the destination *attempted*.)

Parts of Speech That Are Emphasized or De-Emphasized

Just

Just can be an adjective or adverb.

20–56

(As adjective)

> "God is just."
> Here we *emphasize* just.

(As adverb)

> "I (just) want you to be happy."
> Here we do *not* emphasize *just*. It modifies the verb *want*.

> "When Mom did the cooking, it was always (just) right."
> Now it modifies the adjective *right*.

> "Marvin was (just) an ordinary guy."
> Again, no emphasis on *just*. It modifies the adjective *ordinary*.

Ago

Ago may be an adjective or adverb, depending on what it modifies.

> It means *earlier than the present time*.

> When used as an *adjective*, the emphasis is on the noun it modifies.

20–57

> "Five centuries (ago), life was very primitive."

When used as an *adverb*, the emphasis is on *ago*:

> "Long ago, we stopped believing that the earth was flat."

You Need

You need occurs again and again, especially in commercial scripts. Keep in mind that the noun that precedes it is further defined by it.

194

20–58

"We have the continuity you <u>need</u> to trust the care of your portfolio to us."

"At Metropolis Mall, you'll find everything you <u>need</u> for your home furnishings.

If need is used as a *transitive verb*, it is not emphasized, unless the object is a *pronoun*:

"If you (need) <u>furnishings</u> for your home, you want to come to Furniture Warehouse." (Noun object)

"I can get you the supplies if you <u>need</u> (them.)" (Pronoun object)

Review this section again and again until you thoroughly understand what to emphasize and de-emphasize. Listen to the examples on the audio tracks, and find your own examples in the speech of others. The correct emphasis will guarantee that your delivery makes sense and that the listener will understand it. With the appropriate amount of dramatic treatment, your interpretation will be interesting, compelling, and clear.

A few basic reminders:

- Ease into most sentences with a low note/weak beat on the first word, unless it begins with a *noun*, an *exclamation*, a *transitional adverb*, a *one-word setting*, or a *demonstrative pronoun*.

- Build the sentence and almost always end with a statement inflection on a strong ending. (Exceptions: *colloquial phrases* and *passive voice*)

- Focus on *nouns* as subjects of the sentence, objects of verbs, or objects of prepositions.

- Always focus on where the phrase/clause/sentence is going to end, or the *destinations*.

- Take your time, and don't be afraid to *pause* and make longer pauses on *transitions*.

- Read smoothly and naturally, without overarticulating anything.

- Be clear and clean with every syllable in every word. Make believe you're speaking to someone who doesn't understand English very well. Try to walk that fine line of speaking clearly without sounding overdone and affected.

Chapter Twenty-One
WORDS THAT FUNCTION AS NOUNS OR VERBS

Several words commonly used in the English language are pronounced with the emphasis on one syllable as *nouns* and on a different syllable as *verbs*. These are words you should know how to pronounce in either application.

The following are examples of the most common words that fit into this category:

Noun	Verb
1. ATtribute	atTRIbute
2. COMbat	comBAT
3. CONduct	conDUCT
4. CONflict	conFLICT
5. CONtest	conTEST
6. CONtract	conTRACT
7. CONtrast	conTRAST
8. DEcrease	deCREASE
9. EScort	esCORT
10. IMpact	imPACT
11. INcrease	inCREASE
12. INsult	inSULT

13. INtrigue   inTRIGUE
14. OBject   obJECT
15. PERmit   perMIT
16. PRESent   preSENT
17. PROceed   proCEED
18. PROgress   proGRESS
19. PROject   proJECT
20. REbel   reBEL
21. REfill   reFILL
22. REfund   reFUND
23. REject   reJECT
24. REpeat   rePEAT
25. SUBject   subJECT
26. SURvey   surVEY
27. SUSpect   susPECT

Note that the emphasis is on the *first* syllable if it is a *noun* and on the *second* if it is a *verb*.

Practice the sentences below, which contain all of the words previously listed:

21–1

1. "Richard has one significant attribute to offer his prospective employer."

   "Richard will attribute his hiring by the company to making a good first impression."

2. "My friend is a highly decorated combat veteran."

   "My friend the veteran has to combat PTSD every day."

3. "The boy was expelled for bad conduct in school."

   "The committee will conduct a hearing to decide if he can ever come back to school."

198

4. "There is a conflict in my mind as to which side I should take."

   "I am conflicted as to which side I should take."

5. "The attractive brunette from Georgia won the beauty contest."

   "The runner-up will contest the results."

6. "The small company from Ohio won the contract to build the new interstate highway."

   "The state will contract the small company from Ohio to build the new interstate highway."

7. "There is a distinct contrast between his work and play habits."

   "If you contrast his work and play habits, you will see a huge difference."

8. "You will notice that there is a huge decrease in retail shopping compared with a few years ago."

   "Shoppers in retail stores will decrease in the coming years."

9. "Jimmy was her escort for the reception."

   "Jimmy will escort her to the reception."

10. "The negative publicity is having a large impact on tourism in my town."

    "The negative publicity will impact tourism this year."

11. "I expect a significant increase in population in the foreseeable future."

    "Population will continue to increase in the foreseeable future."

12. "The insult from his boss left him in shock."

    "When he was insulted by his boss, it left him in shock."

13. "The story of his intrigue with his mistress intrigued his wife's friends."

14. "He removed the object from the showcase."

"I object to the use of force in this case."

15. "If you want to build a porch, you'll need a permit."

"You may want to build a porch, but the city may not permit it."

16. "I bought my friend a present to show my gratitude."

"I will present my friend with a gift to show my gratitude."

17. "They couldn't wait to divide up the proceeds from the sale."

"They will proceed with the sale of the property."

18. "This company has made a lot of progress this year."

"This company will really progress this year."

19. "Richard is always working on a project."

"Richard projects a stunning year for his new company."

20. "Daisy was always a rebel when it came to dealing with customs and authority."

"Daisy always rebels at customs and authority."

21. "When our doctor writes a prescription, he always includes six months of refills."

"The pharmacy won't refill a prescription unless the doctor includes them in the prescription."

22. "The television he bought was defective, so he demanded a refund."

"The store will refund his money."

23. "The veteran player is a reject from an inferior team."

"The inferior team will reject the veteran player."

24. "The failure of this year's event is a repeat of last year's disappointment."

"The failure of this year's event repeats last year's disappointment."

25. "In the discussion by the disciplinary committee, George's misdeeds will be the main subject."

"The disciplinary committee will subject George to much discussion about his misdeeds."

26. "The researcher will conduct a survey of conflicting opinions by the focus group."

"The researcher will survey the situation to assess conflicting opinions by the focus group."

27. "The doctor is the only suspect in the murder case."

"The authorities only suspect the doctor in the murder case."

Commit these words to memory over a few weeks, as these are all commonly used words that you need to know.

Chapter Twenty-Two
MOST OFTEN MISPRONOUNCED WORDS

Please read this chapter very carefully. Almost *everyone*, including this writer, mispronounces or has mispronounced at least *some* of the words on this list.

If you are working for a high-profile client for the first time, such as a top producer from National Geographic, Discovery Channel, or PBS; an audiobook publisher; or someone else at this level, and you fail to correctly pronounce a number of significant words on this list, either while reading in session from a script or in conversation with them early on, you will most certainly leave an unfavorable impression.

Each word is listed in the left column, the incorrect pronunciation in the middle column, and the correct pronunciation in the right column. All these words are pronounced both incorrectly and correctly on the accompanying audio tracks.

22–1

As listed:	Incorrectly pronounced as:	Correctly pronounced as:
accessible	uh-SES-uh-bul	ak-SES-uh-bul
accessory	uh-SES-uh-ree	ak-SES-uh-ree
accompanist	uh-KUHM-puh-nee-ist	uh-KUHM-puh-nist

across	a-KROST	a-KROSS
actor	AK-tor	AK-tur
accuracy	AK-ur-uh-see	AK-yur-uh-see
adieu	uh-DOO	uh-DYOO
affidavit	af-i-DAY-vid	af-i-DAY-vit
albeit	ALL-bee-it	all-BEE-it
algae	Al-jay	Al-jee
already	aw-RED-ee	awl-RED-ee
alumnae	uh-LUHM-nay	uh-LUHM-nee
Alzheimer's (disease)	OLD Timer's	AHLZ-hy-murz
ambience	AHM-bee-ohnts	AM-bee-ints
amenable	uh-MEN-uh-bul	uh-MEE-nuh-bul
America(n)	uh-MEH-rih-ka(n)	uh-MAH-rih-ka(n)
and	'n'	and
anticlimactic	an-tee-kly-MA-tik	an-tee-kly-MAK-tik
Arctic (and Antarctic)	AR-tik	ARK-tik
ask	aks	ask
asterisk	AS-ter-ik	AS-ter-isk
athlete (athletics)	ATH-uh-leet (ath-uh-LET-iks)	ATH-leet (ath-LET-iks)
Australia	Ost-RAY-yuh	Ost-RAYL-ya
auxiliary	awg-ZIL-uh-ree	awg-ZIL-yuh-ree
balk	BAWLK	BAWK
barbiturate	bar-BIT-u-it	bar-BIT-u-rit
barbed wire	bob-WAR (redneck)	barbd-WYRE
because	bee-KOSS (regional)	bee-KOZ
business	BID-ness	BIZ-ness
cache	cash-AY	CASH
candidate	CAN-ni-date	CAN-di-date

cacophony	caw-CA-fony	cah-CAW-fony
career	KREAR	Kuh-REAR
cavalry	KAL-va-ry	KA-val-ry
chest of drawers	chester DRAWS	chest of DRAWS
clothes	KLOEZE	KLOETHZ
comparable	com-PARE-a-bul	KOM-pahr-a-bul
(also incomparable)		
comptroller	kump-TROE-lur	kum-TROE-lur
contemplative	KAHN-tum-play-tiv	kun-TEM-pluh-tiv
cornet	ko-ro-NET	kor-NET
cosmos	KAHS-mose	KAHS-mus
couldn't	KOOD-int	KOOD-nt
	(No vowel pronounced between *d* and *nt*)	
create	KRATE	kree-AYT
crème de menthe	kreem-duh-MENTH	krem-duh-MAHNT
culinary	KYOO-lin-a-ree	KULL-in-a-ree
decrepit	de-KREP-id	de-KREP-it
demur	di-MYOOR	di-MUR
diction	DIK-shin	DIK-shn
didn't	DID-int	DID-nt
	(No vowel pronounced between d and nt)	
dilate	DI-a-layt	DI-layt
dilapidated	di-LAP-i-tay-tid	di-LAP-i-day-tid
diphtheria	dip-THEER-ee-uh	dif-THEER-ee-uh
dog-eat-dog	doggy DOG	dog-eet-DOG
drowned	DROWN-ded	DROWND
double u (w)	DUB-ya	DUBBLE-you
electoral	i-lek-TOR-ul	i-LEK-tur-ul
entertainment	ehn-nuhr-TAYN-mnt	ehn-tuhr-TAYN-mnt
epoch	EP-awk	EP-uk
escape	ek-SKAYP	e-SKAYP

eschew	e-SHOO, e-SKYOO	es-CHOO
especially	eks-SPESH-uh-lee	e-SPESH-uh-lee
espresso	ek-SPRES-oh	es-PRES-oh
(very common)		
et cetera	ek-SET-uh-ruh	et-SET-uh-ruh
(very common)		
ethos	ETH-ahs	EE-thas
extraordinary	ex-truh-OR-din-air-ree	ex-TROR-din-air-ree
February	FEB-yoo-wa-ree	FEB-roo-wa-ree
	(Almost *everyone* pronounces this incorrectly)	
federal	FED-ruhl	FED-uh-ruhl
(common)		
field	FEE-uhld	FEELD
film	FILL-uhm	FILLM
fiscal	FIZ-i-kuhl	FIS-kuhl
flaccid	FLAS-id	FLAK-sid
foliage	FOE-lij	FOE-lee-ij
formidable	for-MID-uh-bul	FOR-mi-duh-bul
for all intents	for all intensive	for all intents
and purposes	purposes	and purposes
forte	FOR-tay	FORT
government	GUV-uhr-mnt	GUV-uhrn-mnt
grocery	GROE-shur-ree	GROE-sree
height	HYDTH	HYT
(common)		
hierarchy	HY-ar-ky	HY-uhr-ar-ky
imagine	a-MAA-jin	ih-MAA-jin
indefatigable	in-di-fu-TEEG-uh-bul	in-di-FAT-i-guh-bul
in parentheses	in-par-EN-the-sis	in par-EN-the-sees
insurance	IN-shur-uns	in-SHUR-uns
isn't	ID-nt IZ-ent	IZ-nt

205

jewelry	JOO-lu-ree	JOO-wuhl-ree
jubilant	JOO-byoo-lint	JOO-bi-lint
just	JIST	JUST
	(common)	
Ku Klux Klan	Kloo Klucks KLAN	Koo-klucks-KLAN
lambaste	lahm-BAST	lahm-BAYST
larynx	LAR-nicks	LAR-inks
libel	LY-a-bl	LY-bl
(common)		
library	LY-beh-ree	LY-breh-ree
masonry	MAY-sun-eh-ree	MAY-sun-ree
mauve	MAWV	MOHV
mayonnaise	MAY-nayz	MAY-uh-nayz
medieval	med-EE-vul	med-ee-EE-vul
memento	mo-MEN-toe	muh-MEHN-toe
meteorology	mee-ter-AHL-uh-jee	mee-tee-ur-AHL-uh-jee
mischievous	mis-CHEE-vee-us	MIS-chi-vus
(very common)		
mustn't	MUSS-int	MUSS-nt
	(No vowel pronounced between *d* and *nt*)	
naïveté	ny-EEV-uh-tee	nah-eev-TAY
narcissism	NAHR-siz-uhm	NAHR-sis-siz-uhm
New Orleans	nyoo-or-LEENZ	nyoo-OR-linz
nuclear	NOO-kyuh-lur	NYOO-klee-ur
nuptial	NUHP-shoo-ul	NUHP-shul
(common)		
obvious(ly)	AWV-ee-us(lee)	AWB-vee-us(lee)
often	AWF-ten	AWF-in
ophthalmologist	ahp-thuh-MAHL-uh-jist	ahf-thul-MAHL-uh-jist
ordinance	OHR-di-nens	OHRD-nens
orient (as verb)	OHR-y-ehn-tayt	OHR-y-ehnt
(common)		

ostensibly	os-TEHN-siv-lee	os-TEHN-sib-lee
other	NUTH-er	OTH-er
particularly	pahr-TIK-yew-lee	pahr-TIK-yew-lahr-lee
peremptory	pree-EHMP-tuh-ree	puhr-EHMP-tuh-ree
peripheral	puh-RIF-ee-uhl	puh-RIF-uh-ruhl
perspiration	prehs-puh-RAY-shin	purs-puh-RAY-shn
potable	PAHT-a-bul	POH-ta-bul
prerogative	puhr-AW-gah-tiv	preh-RAHG-a-tiv
prescription	puhr-SCRIP-shin	preh-SCRIP-shn
pollute	PLOOT	puh-LOOT
probably	PRAWB-lee	PRAW-bub-lee
pronunciation (common)	pruh-nown-see-AY-shin	pruh-nuhn-see-AY-shn
prostate	PRAH-strayt	PRAH-stayt
realtor	REE-luh-tur	REEL-tur
regardless (common)	ih-reh-GARD-less	reh-GARD-less
relevant	REH-veh-lent	REL-eh-vnt
recur(ing) (common)	ree-oh-KURR(ing)	ree-KURR(ing)
resources	RE-zore-sez	RE-sore-sez
respite	ruh-SPYT	RES-pit
Roosevelt	ROOZ-uh-velt	ROH-zuh-velt
schizophrenia	skit-suh-FREN-ee-uh	skit-suh-FREE-nee-uh
school	SKOO-wuhl (common)	SKOOL
sherbet	SHUR-burt (common)	SHUR-bit
shouldn't	SHOOD-int (No vowel pronounced between *d* and *nt*)	SHOOD-nt
silicon	SILL-kon	SIL-ih-kun

sneaked (fairly common)	SNUCK	SNEEKD
so	SOEZ	SOE
spit and image	spitting image	spit and image
subsidiary	sub-SID-uh-rer-ree	sub-SID-ee-eh-ree
succinct(ly)	suh-SINGKT(ly)	suhk-SINGKT(ly)
suite	SOOT	SWEET
supposedly	suh-POES-uh-blee	suh-POES-zed-lee
supremacist	soo-PREHM-ist (common)	soo-PREHM-uh-sist
tact	TACK	TAKT
temperature	TEM-pur-chur	TEM-pur-uh-chur
tenant	TEH-neht	TEHN-uhnt
tenterhooks	TEHN-duhr-hooks	TEHN-tuhr-hooks
Tijuana (common)	tee-ya-WAHN-a	tee-WAHN-a
tin	TEHN	TIHN
triathlon (common)	try-ATH-a-lon	try-ATH-lon
unequivocally	uhn-i-KWIV-uh-kuh-blee	uhn-i-KWIV-uh-kuh-lee
utmost	UHP-mohst	UHT-mohst
verbiage (very common)	VUR-bij	VUR-bee-ij
voluptuous	vah-LUMP-choo-us	voh-LUP-choo-us
wasn't	WAHD-nt	WAHZ-nt
wouldn't	WOOD-int	WOOD-nt
yolk	YOKE (common)	YOELK
zoology (very common)	zoo-AW-luh-ji	zoe-AW-luh-ji

Another observation:

Over the years, I have observed a significant number of people pronouncing *s* as *sh* in front of *t*, *tr*, and occasionally *ch*.

22–2

(As written)	(Incorrect)	(Correct)
strange	shtraynj	straynj
strong	shtrohng	strohng
school	shkool	skool

Make every effort to master your pronunciation of these words, as most of them are used often in conversation and in the written word. There are others, but only the more *often* mispronounced words have been listed here.

Chapter Twenty-Three
Numbers and Colors

Numbers and colors are *nouns*; when they modify, they are *adjectives*. In general, numbers as nouns are *emphasized*, and numbers as adjectives are *not*, except in comparing/contrasting situations.

Numbers

Emphasize the number(s) as *nouns*.

23–1

"The number <u>seven</u> is considered to be a lucky number."

"Look for 20<u>20</u> as the address of my ophthalmologist on Iris Drive."

(Or)

"Look for 2020 Iris <u>Drive</u> as the address of my ophthalmologist." (The word *Drive* is now the destination.)

"Twenty-<u>one</u> is the defining age of adulthood."

"<u>One</u>, <u>two</u>, <u>three</u>, <u>four</u>, <u>five</u>, <u>six</u>, <u>seven</u>, <u>eight</u>, <u>nine</u>, <u>ten</u>."

Emphasize the *noun*, not the number used as an *adjective*.

23–2

"There are (three) <u>trumpets</u>, (three) <u>trombones</u>, (four) <u>French horns</u>, and (one) <u>tuba</u> in most symphony orchestras."

"Joe has been married (three) <u>times</u>."

"I've heard this story in a (thousand) different <u>versions</u>." (*Thousand* could also be emphasized for dramatic effect.)

"You must be over <u>eighteen</u> (implied *years old*) to be able to drink in a public place." (Here, the emphasis is on eighteen without the phrase *years old*.)

STREET NUMBERS

These are *adjectives*. Emphasize the *noun*.

23–3

"(*1600*) Pennsylvania <u>Avenue</u>"

"(*10*) <u>Downing</u> Street"

"(*108*) <u>State</u> Street"

"(*1222*) Sunset <u>Boulevard</u>"

PHONE NUMBERS

Many radio and television commercials contain a phone number to call. Each group of numbers should be treated as a declarative sentence, with the emphasis on the last number.

(Note that many radio and television ads have shifted to the *Internet*, where sites such as YouTube and Pandora contain advertising messages. In addition, a significant percentage of ads now use website references instead of phone numbers.)

23–4

"1-31<u>2</u>-27<u>1</u>-982<u>6</u>"

With the area code, the entire phone number is broken into *three* parts, not four, as the one in front of the area code is considered to be part of the area code grouping:

"(1-20<u>2</u>)-76<u>2</u>-882<u>1</u>" (one two oh <u>two</u>)

With seven hundred or eight hundred numbers:

"(1-800)-29<u>0</u>-550<u>5</u>" (one eight hundred)

"(1–87<u>7</u>)-65<u>5</u>-80<u>9</u>0" (we emphasize nine because it is contrasting with 8)

"(1–78<u>8</u>)-78<u>1</u>-9<u>000</u>" ("9000" is pronounced as nine-<u>thousand</u>)

"(1–88<u>8</u>)-62<u>9</u>-8200 ("8200" is pronounced as eighty-two <u>hundred</u> or eight two <u>hundred</u>)

OMITTING *AND*

With numbers over one hundred, do not use the conjunction *and* in the number. (Most people do this.)

Here are several examples:

<u>23–5</u>

	Incorrect	Correct
172	One hundred and seventy-two	One hundred seventy-two
5010	Five thousand and ten	Five thousand ten
755,000	Seven hundred and fifty-five thousand	Seven hundred fifty-five thousand
8,004,040	Eight million, four thousand and forty	Eight million four thousand forty

Several examples ahead further illustrate omission of the *and*.

LARGE NUMBERS

When voicing a large number, divide the larger number into groups of three, beginning at the far right of the number in this order:

Trillions—billions—millions—thousands—hundreds

The last group to the right breaks down, further, from left to right: hundreds, tens, units.

Here are progressive examples of very small to very large numbers and how to deliver them:

23–6

9 feet	nine feet
29 feet	twenty-nine feet
129 feet	one-hundred twenty-nine feet
	(do not say *and* twenty-nine feet)
8,129 feet	eight-thousand one-hundred twenty-nine feet
48,129 feet	Forty-eight thousand, one-hundred twenty-nine feet
748,129 feet	Seven hundred forty-eight thousand one-hundred twenty-nine feet
1,748,129 feet	One million seven hundred forty-eight thousand one hundred twenty-nine feet
51,748,129 feet	Fifty-one million seven hundred, etc.
651,748,129 feet	Six hundred fifty-one million, etc.
3,651,748,129 feet	Three billion, six hundred fifty-one million, etc.
93,651,748,129 feet	Ninety-three billion, six hundred, etc.
493,651,748,129 feet	Four hundred ninety-three billion, etc.
1,493,651,748,129 feet	One trillion, four hundred ninety-three billion, etc.

When analyzing the number, always work backward from the right, and remember that hundreds change to thousands to millions to billions to trillions in groups of three. These groups are almost always divided by commas, especially when the number is in the tens of thousands (five digits).

For each group of three, the numbers are pronounced exactly the same as in the *hundreds* group, with the exception that it is followed by thousand, million, billion, or trillion for the respective group it represents.

23–7

Hundreds:

9   (nine)
29   (twenty-nine)
129   (one-hundred twenty-nine)

Thousands:

8   (eight thousand)
48   (forty-eight thousand)
748   (seven hundred forty-eight thousand)

Millions:

1   (one million)
51   (fifty-one million)
651   (six hundred fifty-one million)

Billions:

3   (three billion)
93   (ninety-three billion)
493   (four hundred ninety-three billion)

Trillions:

1   (one trillion)
(and so forth)

Reassemble the groups, and once again, we have one trillion, four hundred ninety-three billion, six hundred fifty-one million, seven hundred forty-eight thousand, one hundred twenty-nine (1,493,651,748,129).

If you have a problem with voicing large numbers, the following is a list of numbers, from very small to very large, for you to practice. Work slowly at first, then gradually speed it up over several practice days.

Do this list in three steps:

1. Read each in order as the number only.

2. Read each in order, and add the word <u>dollars</u>.

3. Read each in order, putting the number in the sentence "Last year, I made _____ dollars."

100	10273	5,681,681
156	10581	10,880,440
178	10777	17,177,771
289	11622	171,777,778
500	11111	338,125,001
600	15281	944,440,449
700	100000	1,000,000,000
1746	100003	1,335,655,014
1500	100033	18,200,000,000
2500	110855	12,888,888,886
2795	265555	485,250,600,555
7470	666666	1,000,000,000,000
10,000	445544	1,666,555,444,350
10,003	1000	18,000,880,770,660,550
10,010	1472	385,665,420,543,213,222
10,100	2047	555,888,444,333,222,111

KEEPING TRACK OF NUMBERS IN A SEQUENCE

When talking about things progressively that have different costs, you must keep track of what has been said in previous sentences so that what you say now <u>compares</u> or <u>contrasts</u> with it.

Here's a good example:

23–8

> "Defense costs are getting way out of hand. The navy's new largest
> carrier will cost fourteen billion <u>dollars</u> (first time). A smaller
> Nimitz-class carrier is expected to cost <u>three</u> billion dollars (second
> time). (Emphasize <u>three</u> a bit more, as it is the first comparison with
> fourteen.) And a new Arleigh <u>Burke</u> class <u>destroyer</u> is expected to
> cost <u>one</u> billion dollars each. (The third time, hit <u>one</u> with gusto, and
> give it a finalizing declarative inflection, as it ends the comparisons.)"

Notice that in the statement of the first cost, we emphasize *dollars*, as
there is, up to this point, no comparison. We are establishing the unit,
dollars.

In the previous example, if the first number were 14.5, the second
number 3.8, and the third number 1.2 billion dollars, the emphasis
would be illustrated like this:

23–9

> "The navy's new largest aircraft carrier will cost 14.5 billion <u>dollars</u>.
> A smaller Nimitz-class carrier is expected to cost <u>3.8</u> billion dollars.
> And a new Arleigh Burke class destroyer is expected to cost <u>1.2</u>
> billion dollars." (3.8 compares with 14.5; 1.2 compares with 3.8.)

You must keep track of what is stated for the first time and what is stated
progressively as you move through the script so you can be aware of
comparisons and contrasts as well as redundancies.

INDEFINITE NUMBERS

One of the most common ways writers convey impressive images
of many people or entities at once is by using *hundreds, thousands,
millions,* and *billions,* followed by the preposition *of,* which leads into
the people or entities described.

23–10

"There were millions of black <u>flies</u> annoying the fishermen on that humid spring night."

"Billions of <u>dollars</u> were wasted in recent wars in the Middle East."

"<u>Thousands</u> of people were killed in the street by the advancing army." (Here, the emphasis is on *thousands* because *people* is treated as a *pronoun*. If you were to emphasize *people*, it might sound as if you were drawing attention to an implied comparison of *people* being killed, as opposed to, say, *animals*.)

"Hundreds of gallons of <u>water</u> poured into the leaking basement." (Emphasis is on <u>water</u>, not gallons; *water* is the focus and the *destination*.)

As with the example of *thousands of people*, if the people or entities described by the indefinite numbers are redundant, then the emphasis will be on hundreds, thousands, millions, or billions.

23–11

"There were black flies everywhere. <u>Millions</u> of them (black flies) annoyed the fishermen."

"The dollars poured out of the government war chest. <u>Billions</u> of them (dollars) were wasted."

"Water poured into the basement, hundreds of <u>gallons</u> of it." (Here, the emphasis is on *gallons*, as it is now the noun of focus, and it is followed by a prepositional phrase going to a *pronoun*.)

STATISTICS

When comparison is used to deliver a *statistic*, there are two approaches.

23–12

1. Concentrate on the *numbers* when no *units* are mentioned:

217

"One in <u>ten</u> will die before the age of sixty-five."

"One out of every <u>six</u> of our subscribers is a millionaire."

2. When *units* are in the sentence, with the numbers modifying them, emphasize the *units*:

"One in seven <u>persons</u> will die of this dreadful disease."

"Four out of five <u>workers</u> make less than ten dollars an hour."

Percentages

When a unit follows a percentage, the emphasis will again be, not on the unit, but on *percent* or *percentages*:

<u>23–13</u>

"Forty-five <u>percent</u> of people in the United States make under twenty-five thousand dollars a year."

"A very large <u>percentage</u> of people make less than twenty-five thousand dollars a year."

Percent can also act as a *preceding adjective*, in which case it is not emphasized. The word it *modifies* is emphasized:

"Solder can consist of 60 (percent) <u>tin</u> and 40 (percent) <u>lead</u>."

Colors

<u>23–14</u>

As nouns:

"<u>Red</u> is my favorite color."

"That shade of <u>blue</u> really appeals to me."

"The fall leaves appeared in the hue of <u>orange</u> and <u>ochre</u>."

As adjectives:

"Adele walked in the <u>Easter</u> Parade in her beautiful (yellow) <u>hat</u>."

"The night <u>sky</u> appeared as a (black) <u>shroud</u> over the <u>city</u>."

"The color of her <u>face</u> changed dramatically from pink to <u>red</u>, as she blushed at the embarrassing <u>remark</u>."

Note that neither *yellow* nor *black* are emphasized, as they are *preceding modifiers*. *Pink* and *red* are emphasized because they are *succeeding* modifiers, which are placed at the *end* of the clause. *Red* gets more emphasis, as it is the one making the comparison.

Noun or Adjective?

Remember that when you encounter one or more numbers or colors in a sentence, the first thing you need to figure out is whether each one is functioning as a *noun* or an *adjective*. This is the first step in discerning where the points of emphasis belong.

As you can see, numbers and colors are frequently compared and contrasted. In keeping with the principle of growing intensity in sentences, the object of comparison or contrast is always the *last* one.

Chapter Twenty-Four
On Marking Scripts

Enough cannot be said about the importance of marking scripts. The most important reason for this is that there is too much at stake for you to lose a client because you assumed you could solely trust your instincts and memory to deliver a script to a client's satisfaction.

In a live session, it is particularly important to mark a script according to whatever corrections and instructions you may receive while being directed by a client. If that client corrects what you are doing at any particular moment in a script and you don't make note of that correction and instead trust your short-term memory to remind you of the correction, you are almost certain to deliver the phrase incorrectly as you did in the first take. This will drive a client to extreme frustration. Frequently, making small notations is often all it takes to avoid this problem.

When you make notes, always make them with a *pencil*. If you do them in ink, the only way you can make a change in the notation is to cross it out and write above it, below it, or in the margins, which will make your script potentially very messy and difficult to read.

Over time, you may develop your own preferences for how you wish to mark a script. In the meantime, let me make the following recommendations:

To *emphasize* certain words, *underline* them, or better yet, if certain words are multisyllabic, underline only the *strong* syllable.

24–1

"Ulysses S. <u>Grant</u> was a scrupulously <u>hon</u>est man."

"Even an <u>am</u>ateur can tell if a narrator doesn't sound pro<u>fess</u>ional."

Note the underline for the strong syllables in *multisyllabic* words.

As a reminder *not* to emphasize a certain word (or phrase), mark under it with a *down* arrow. This is particularly helpful with remembering words that are *redundant*.

24–2

"He loved Anita deeply from the time they met. Surprisingly, late in life, after countless financial squabbles, he <u>left</u> Anita."
(The second *Anita* is *redundant*.)   V

"He gives willingly to the <u>Blood</u> Bank every year."

                                    V

(*Blood Bank* is a *compound noun*, so *Bank* is marked to be de-emphasized.)

For a pause between words, phrases, and clauses, draw a *vertical line*. In the case of a long pause, as in a transition, draw *two* parallel vertical lines:

24–3

"At the age of <u>thirty-one</u>, | Joe fell into <u>depression</u>, | just as his <u>father</u> had at this age many years <u>earlier</u>."
(Here, pauses are inserted where the *commas* are, but also for *dramatic enhancement* of the last phrase.)

24–4

"Thus an <u>era</u> ended with the close of the <u>Gilded</u> Age. │ │ At the beginning of World War <u>II</u>, Americans were on their way to a more <u>equitable</u> economic <u>footing</u>."

(Long pause indicating a *transition*, indicated by a *double* line.)

As a reminder to pitch *up* a word or syllable, draw an arrow pointing up *over* the word or strong syllable:

24–5

∧   ∧   ∧   ∧
"<u>Tony</u> was a good <u>boy</u>, and his <u>parents</u> were <u>proud</u> of him."
     ∨   ∨ ∨

(Here pitching up *Tony*, *boy*, *parents*, and *proud* enhances the dramatic push of the sentence.)

∧   ∧   ∧
"<u>Wow</u>! Look at the <u>size</u> of that giant <u>panda</u>!"
          ∨ ∨

(*Wow*, *size*, and *panda* cry out for pitching up to enhance the excitement of seeing the huge panda.)

As a reminder to pitch *down* a word or syllable, draw an arrow pointing down *under* the word or syllable:

24–6

          ∧   ∧
"There was no getting <u>around</u> the problem. They were <u>lost</u>."
∨   ∨ ∨ ∨

(*They* and *were* are pitched down, for the purpose of putting all the dramatic attention on *lost*.)

     ∧   ∧
"He was an <u>evil</u> man. A lying, deceiving, <u>manipulative</u> man."
     ∨   ∨

Here, *man* in both cases is redundant, since each stands for *he*. *Evil* and *manipulative* are pitched up. *Man* is pitched down. Note that the upward marker is over the strong syllable.

24–7

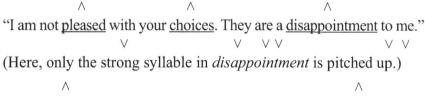

"I am not <u>pleased</u> with your <u>choices</u>. They are a <u>disappointment</u> to me."

(Here, only the strong syllable in *disappointment* is pitched up.)

    ∧   ∧

"After <u>months</u> of observing your actions with me and <u>others</u>, I have

                             ∧   ∧

come to the inescapable conclusion that <u>you</u> are my <u>enemy</u>."

                            ∨   ∨ ∨

(Special emphasis on *you* to single it out as the object of my distrust. Downplaying *are* and *my* sets up *enemy*.)

Remember to build intensity in a list, phrase, or clause. This is not about increasing volume. It is about increasing *intensity*.

24–8

                                               ∧

"The dreams, | the hopes, | the ideals, | the very <u>promise</u> of good

∧   ∧

<u>ideas</u> | transformed into reality."

    ∨   ∨

               ∧   ∧   ∧   ∧

"He was narrow-minded, | insensitive, | shallow, | and <u>unrepentant</u>."

                                           ∨

Again, note the markings over the strong syllables, as well as vertical lines that represent pauses. Observe also the underline (for emphasis, this time) on *the last item in the list*.

Always have a pencil at the ready when you are working either alone or with a producer or director. It's the mark of a professional. (No pun intended.)

Chapter Twenty-Five
ABOUT PRACTICING

D o *not* do the same thing over and over again and expect different results. Instead, you must try new approaches, experiment with your emotions, and alter every parameter of what you are doing in your efforts to effectively interpret scripts.

The Four Stages of Learning

The learning process has often been sabotaged because of the feelings of inadequacy people experience when they make mistakes in learning a new skill.

Ironically, making mistakes and not doing it right are vital steps in the learning process. Yet too often we focus our attention on avoiding the bad feelings rather than on learning the task. Understanding the four stages of learning a skill can help keep you focused on what works for you. The following are the Four Stages of Learning, according to Abraham Maslow:

1. **Unconscious Incompetence**

You don't know that you don't know how to do this. This is the stage of blissful ignorance before learning begins.

2. Conscious Incompetence

You *know* that you don't know how to do this, at this point in time. This is where learning begins and where the most negative judgments against yourself are formed. This is also the stage where most people give up.

3. Conscious Competence

You now know that you *know* how to do this. Although this stage of learning is a relief from the second stage, you are nevertheless still self-conscious and somewhat uneasy with it.

4. Unconscious Competence

In this stage, the skill you have learned now comes naturally to you. It has become *habitual*.

If it has been determined that you have talent and ability, if you are working with a competent instructor, and if you practice faithfully and diligently, your progress will be very evident within a few months. If you work alone, it will take longer—often a great deal longer.

If you are new to voice over acting, depending on your professional and personal schedule, you should try to allow a half hour each weekday to practice with scripts and, if possible, to do an hour on Saturday. If you can do an hour a day during the week, so much the better. Take Sunday off. Or if you practice Sunday, take Saturday off. You don't need to practice every day of the week.

If you live in an area where you can't find a good one-on-one instructor, try finding one who offers online instruction. It's not quite the same as being in the room with the instructor, but it's a pretty effective second choice, especially if you live a good distance from a major metropolitan area.

Here are some steps you can take at home to improve your delivery. You can also do them as an add-on to your instruction, if you are working with or have worked with a coach.

1. Record selected commercials or narrations from YouTube, radio, or television. Most TVs have a direct audio output that can be connected to a CD recorder or input to a computer. Pick out those performances that you think will fit your voice and personality. Vary the content from selection to selection. Pick out pieces that challenge you. You won't learn more by working on material you already do well.

2. Play back each selection and transcribe it, so that you will have a working script of it.

3. Listen to the original performance several times, then try it yourself, making every effort to *imitate* the performance in every detail—in flow, timing, inflection, pitch, phrasing, mood, timbre, emotion, pace, etc.

4. Now record your performance and play it back. Listen carefully and critically to discern the similarities and differences between your performance and the original that you recorded from the TV. The first and most basic consideration should be, "Am I into it? Am I believable? Does it sound as if it's *my* message and no one else's? Am I giving it the proper emotion and focus? Am I overdoing it? *Underdoing* it?" Mark the script according to your observations.

5. Rerecord the script and apply your corrections, then play it back as before. Observe the *new* results. Any improvement? Refine it further, as before, rerecord it, and play it back. This is the process.

The next time you practice, repeat the process with the previous script from the last practice session. Then add a new script, and start the process all over again. Once you feel that you've exhausted the usefulness of previous scripts, move ahead with new material. Over a month or so, depending on length, you could be learning from ten to twenty performances.

You may also find it useful to perform in *unison* with the original performance. This will give you a good sense of pace, pause, phrasing, and hopefully emotional content. Be sure to turn up the volume so that the playback is as loud in your ear as your own voice when you are reading the script with the recorded performance.

When you play your recorded voice back, don't worry about how you think you sound. What matters is how *believable* you are. Would what you are saying in the script move you as a listener if it were someone else talking to you? Since practice inevitably involves getting rid of bad habits and creating good ones, it is important that you keep this concept on your mind as often as possible. If you're having difficulty with a word, phrase, or sentence, go over it at every opportunity until it's very natural and comfortable to you.

Remember also that if you have trouble with pronunciation, emphasis, pitch, timing, or flow of a word or short phrase, the worst approach you can make is to keep going back to the beginning of the phrase, clause, or sentence containing it and reading from the beginning. You will simply be reinforcing the problem. Instead, carefully correct the problem on the word or phrase first, then read while adding the word ahead of it, then read while adding the word that follows it, and gradually expand progressively outward in both directions until the entire phrase flows smoothly and easily. Slowing the pace can help, as can quasi-singing the phrase that is giving you trouble.

As you practice, try to continuously think about the message—what it *means*, how you relate it to *real life*, how you would deliver it in a real situation (or how someone might speak it to you), what visual *setting* the message evokes, and what *emotions* the message must generate from you.

Get an image of the listener in your mind. Always feel his or her presence when you speak the script. Remember, although the script has been written by someone else, in reality, it's *your* message.

Take your time. Relax. This works best when you demonstrate a very active, fanciful, imaginative, imitative, inspired mind, and a comfortably relaxed, loose-feeling body.

Don't be reluctant to *pause*. The pause is a powerful dramatic weapon. Making good use of it also allows you to think ahead and plan out the phrase, clause, or sentence that follows each moment of delivery. Don't let the words you're delivering get ahead of your brain. It takes practice to reach the full realization of just how much time you have to deliver the script and to understand that you have more than ample room to pause.

Experiment with widening the pitch range of the delivery. Try overplaying or underplaying it, and then listen back to the results. Do you sound real? Believable? Natural? Would you believe the genuineness of the delivery if you were the audience? At some point in time, you will become your own best critic. However, stay positive. If you make mistakes, and you will—*lots* of them—don't beat yourself up. Use your mistakes as a potent learning tool.

Every time you open your mouth to deliver a phrase, ask yourself, "How would I say this to someone in real life? How would they say it to me?" Get inside your listener's head, and try to think in terms of the way he or she expects to hear what you have to say. It's ultimately all about drawing from your observations in real life.

To improve your cold-reading ability, try to read a paragraph or two of fresh material every day as part of your practice. As you do this, try to read it smoothly and comfortably. If you make a mistake, just keep going. Remember that the purpose of this exercise is to get you in the habit of reading evenly without stopping. If you can master this over a wide range of material, and do it with few errors, you will be very confident and comfortable about your reading ability.

Become a keen observer of the differences in speech patterns and personalities of all kinds of people, of the ways some people make a profound impression on you through their verbal communication skills, and of the ways in which others fall short. Develop the habit of examining every detail that affects your understanding of the meaning of what people say and your reaction to how they say it. Remember, it's about *talking*, not about *reading*. The people who listen to your voice over performances should never sense that you're *reading* to them.

Chapter Twenty-Six
PRACTICE SCRIPTS

Commercials

<u>26–1</u>

Mall—*Madison Mall*

Everything you've dreamed about and more, at the new Madison Mall! A world of shopping awaits you! Macy's, Neiman-Marcus, Saks Jandel, Nordstrom's, Prada, and a collection of specialty stores that will amaze you! And we have acres of free parking and for your convenience, valet parking! And fourteen of the best restaurants in town. Come experience shopping as you've never known it. Madison Mall! Innovative shopping at its best! Just off exit sixteen off I-45 in North Hastings.

<u>26–2</u>

Retail—*Beverly's Boutique*

Shop smart at Beverly's Boutique in downtown Boca Raton! Try on our one-of-a-kind designer dresses. Match it up with one of our imported custom scarves and our full line of colorful, unique designer shoes. You can buy that distinctive outfit with the assurance that it is one of a kind. We *guarantee* it! Beverly's Boutique, in downtown Boca Raton. Call 561-368-6500.

26–3

The Arts—*Canadian Brass*

Spend a wild and zany musical evening with the Canadian Brass as they perform music from their two new albums, *Swingtime* and *Basin Street*, featuring surprise guest performances by four of America's jazz greats. The Canadian Brass, performing at the Kennedy Center Concert Hall, Saturday evening, March 11, and Sunday matinee at three. Don't miss it! For tickets, go to ticketmaster.com or call 844-753-8364.

26–4

Car Dealer Soft Sell—*Longly Lexus*

Twenty years ago, we set out to offer our customers the world's best automobiles at a fair price, with all the amenities, and offer superior attention and service that would surpass all our competition. Through the years, that business philosophy has worked well for us and for our discriminating customers, who know that in the end, when it comes to buying a Lexus, it's simply a matter of good…or *superior*. Longly Lexus—Nashville's *best*.

26–5

Car Dealer Medium Sell—*Northridge Toyota*

At Northridge Toyota, we're having a once-a-year sale that will blow you away. Hundreds of Corollas, Camrys, RAV 4s, and Highlanders, at the lowest prices of the year. No money down, with 0 percent financing for up to five years on the model and color of your choice. Don't miss this chance to save like never before on this one-time opportunity at Northridge Toyota, in Northridge Auto Park. Come on over today.

26–6

Hard Sell—*Furniture World*

This is it! The opportunity of a lifetime! Your one chance to save a bundle! This weekend, and this weekend only, Furniture World is offering entire rooms of furniture at unbelievable rock-bottom prices! Breakfronts; armoires; marble-top commodes; breakfast, living room, and bedroom sets; and much more! Only at Furniture World, on the northeast corner of Emerson Auto Park! Doors open at 7:00 a.m.! Get here early, because the best deals are going fast! Don't miss out!

26–7

PSA 1—*Boys and Girls Clubs PSA*

He was my greatest inspiration. A giant. A great heart. Loving and compassionate to everyone he worked with. Dick Dawkins. He ran the Boys and Girls Club in my town when I was a kid. He was my motivator and still is. He helped a lot of kids get their act together. If there's a Boys and Girls Club in your town, chances are there's a Dick Dawkins there, too. Give generously to your local Boys and Girls Club. For more information, go to boysandgirlsclubs.com.

26–8

PSA 2—*Smoke Alarm PSA*

If a fire breaks out in your home and you and your family are asleep, what will you do? Answer: Probably nothing, because it'll be too late. A working smoke alarm would have warned you of the first sign of danger, and you and your family would have had plenty of time to get out. Be sure you have working smoke alarms in your home. To learn more, go to smokealarm.com.

26–9

Business/Financial—*Vanguard*

As one of the world's largest investment companies, with more than three billion dollars in assets globally, Vanguard has been at the forefront of index funds for individual investors ever since it developed the world's first index fund for individual investors in 1976.

In today's markets, Vanguard offers the finest and broadest offerings in the industry that contain virtually all sectors of the domestic and worldwide stock and bond markets, all at significant cost-savings to the investor, reflecting the fact that Vanguard is owned by its clients. Its profits go directly to you, the client. Isn't that how the investing experience should be? For more information, call us at 1-877-662-7447.

26–10

Hospitality/Restaurant—***The Columbia Continental Restaurant***

Indulge yourself in splendor at the Columbia Continental Restaurant, where the setting is historic, the cuisine is sumptuous, and the grandeur is ageless.

The Columbia Continental offers originality and distinction in its one-of-a-kind menu, as well as its famous five-star service. And you'll love the view of the lake from our outdoor dining terrace. Come and savor the finest continental cuisine at the Columbia Continental Restaurant, an experience you'll long remember. Call 1-800-481-4200 for reservations.

26–11

Hospitality/Hotel—***Waldorf Towers***

If you're in New York on a business trip, you'll want to make the Waldorf Towers your home away from home. Enter into your beautifully appointed executive guest room and individually decorated suites through our private entrance and lobby. And, of course, you'll experience our legendary impeccable service, unmatched anywhere. Enjoy luxury at its finest at the Towers of the Waldorf Astoria. For reservations, go to booking.com or call 1-212-355-3100.

26–12

Internet—*CenturyLink*

You're a small business owner with a great idea, solid growth, and a bright future ahead. You've had a good working Internet service, but now you need a high-speed service and voice bundle. CenturyLink can do it all. We can help you work smarter and save more in the process. You can lock in a great rate with a two-year term, and as your business grows, you can increase your Internet speed and stay cost-effective. You'll also get Microsoft Office 365, data backup, and web hosting, with no add-on charge. Go to CenturyLink.com for more information.

26–13

Hospitality/Resort—*The Hawaii Six*

Six secluded sanctuaries. The Royal Hawaiian, a classic resort on Waikiki Beach. Kea Lani Villas and Suites on Kaua'i. On the big island of Hawaii, the Orchid at Mauna Lani, your private retreat in the land of the volcano. The Lodge at Koele, voted one of *Travel and Leisure* readers' Best Beach hotels. Manele Bay Hotel, set atop a lava cliff overlooking the Pacific Ocean. And last, the Kapalua Bay Hotel on Maui, with seemingly eternal sunsets. These five-star resorts recall traveling's golden age, when service was impeccable and you were pampered beyond your wildest dreams. Come to Hawaii's best. For more information, go to thehawaiisix.com.

Narrations

26–14

Business—*Answering the Challenges*

Today, in a changing economic climate, owners recognize the continuing need for competent contractors and skilled craftsmen operating in a stable labor-relations climate, but they now expect a firm price with quality work, completed on budget and on time. This new climate has led to an open-shop movement that has more than doubled in the last ten years, and which represents major challenges to both union contractors and building trade unions.

To answer these challenges, we offer a distinctive set of services from a special organization of skilled union workers, with the assurance that you can count on the work we do to be delivered as promised.

26–15

Documentary—*The End in Vietnam*

After years of bloody fighting and endless bomb strikes, the United States and North Vietnam signed a cease-fire agreement on January 27, 1973, in Paris. "We have finally achieved peace with honor," President Nixon was quoted.

In America, however, there was no celebration in the streets. Americans by this time were apathetic to a war that had lasted over ten years and cost the nation its belief in its invulnerability and the loss of almost sixty thousand of its young lives.

In spite of the costly efforts of its assumed vastly superior military, America had to resign itself to a Communist takeover of Vietnam.

26–16

Biography—*Albert Einstein*

A German-born theoretical physicist, Albert Einstein is known as the developer of the theory of relativity, which, along with quantum mechanics, formed the pillars of modern physics.

In 1933, when Hitler came to power, Einstein was visiting the United States and did not return to his home country, where he had been a professor at the Berlin Academy of Sciences.

At the beginning of World War II, he endorsed a letter to FDR, which persuaded him to begin research on "extremely powerful bombs of a new type," as he put it, which later became the Manhattan Project.

Einstein always supported the defense of allied forces but was adamantly against the use of nuclear fission as a destructive weapon, and with his friend Bertrand Russell, made his intentions public.

He published over 300 scientific and over 150 nonscientific works. He is considered by most to be the greatest scientific mind of the twentieth century.

26–17

Biography—*Elizabeth Cady Stanton*

No one is more consequential to the creation and implementation of women's rights than Elizabeth Cady Stanton. A passionate social activist, she initiated the first organized women's rights movements in the United States. Prior to focusing mainly on the rights of women, she and her husband, Henry, were active abolitionists.

After the Civil War, Stanton and Susan B. Anthony withdrew support for the Fourteenth and Fifteenth Amendments to the US Constitution because the amendments would give more legal protection and voting rights to African American men while denying those rights to black and white women. Her dedication to these issues, as well as to women's rights beyond the right to vote, led to the formation of two landmark women's rights organizations, and when they were joined together as one movement, she was elected president of the combined confederation.

As the keynote speaker at the Women's Suffrage Convention in Washington, DC, in 1868, she delivered a commanding speech, which began with a rebuke of man as destroyer in the lives of ordinary Americans: "I urge a sixteenth amendment, because 'manhood suffrage,' or a man's government, is civil, religious, and social disorganization. The male element is a destructive force, stern, selfish, aggrandizing, loving war, violence, conquest, acquisition, breeding in the material and moral world alike discord, disorder, disease, and death. See what a record of blood and cruelty the pages of history reveal! Through what slavery, slaughter, and sacrifice, through what inquisitions and imprisonments, pains and persecutions, black codes and gloomy creeds, the soul of humanity has struggled for the centuries, while mercy has veiled her face and all hearts have been dead alike to love and hope!"

26–18

Historical—*Eighteenth Century European Music Transition*

Two distinct eras of musical style predominated in the eighteenth century: baroque and classical. Originated in Italy in the early seventeenth century, the baroque style persisted throughout Europe through the middle of the eighteenth century.

The baroque style embodied the concept of tonality, an approach in which a song or instrumental composition is written in a particular key. Baroque music expanded the size, range, and complexity of instrumental performance and also established the vocal and instrumental forms of opera, cantata, and oratorio. Major composers of this period include Bach, Handel, Purcell, Monteverdi, and Scarlatti.

The classical style, in contrast, has a lighter, clearer texture than baroque and is less complex. Also, in this period, the harpsichord was replaced by the piano. Variety and contrast within a composition became more pronounced than in the baroque era, and the orchestra increased in size, range, and power. The best-known composers of the classical era are Beethoven, Haydn, Mozart, and Schubert.

26–19

Travel—*Galapagos Islands*

The Galapagos Islands were described by Charles Darwin as "eminently curious." The archipelago is comprised of thirteen islands and more than a hundred islets. Since the islands are volcanic, their coastlines look more like moonscapes.

There is teeming life all over the Galapagos, and almost two hundred species are found nowhere else in the world. These species evolved all by themselves before human life arrived in the late fifteenth century.

Approximately 90 percent of these unique species still remain, but there is great debate about how long they will continue to survive. Exhaustive efforts by international conservation groups and new environmental laws passed by the Ecuadorian government inspire hope that this unique ecosystem will continue to thrive into the future.

26–20

Commentary Nonfiction—***Make Room For Man***

Be fruitful and multiply…

Throughout the twentieth century and to the present day, man has increasingly followed this biblical directive to a fault, to the point where our very presence is an ominous threat to all other life forms on the planet, including our own.

In the years between 1950 and 2000, an already swelling population of humans on the earth more than *doubled*. Think about that for a moment. Just two hundred years ago, the population of the earth totaled just over a billion. Today, there are over *seven* billion people on the planet. In all of man's time on earth, a growth spurt of that magnitude, in those huge numbers, was never even considered to be possible. (Malthus, of course, thought otherwise.) It is now predicted to increase 30 percent from 2000 to 2025.

Moreover, from 1950 to the present time, over 25 percent of animals and plants on the earth became extinct. Most authorities on extinction agree that a far larger percentage of the remaining species is in danger of the same fate over the next twenty to thirty years. There is already abundant dialogue about eradication of species in the wild whose presence we have always taken for granted: elephants, lions, tigers, gorillas, sea mammals, large fish (and the fish they eat), and polar bears. A conservative estimate of the full number in peril is as much as 50 percent of all the species now living on the earth.

The fact that scientists are even considering species' priorities for survival is in itself alarming.

Is man responsible for this precipitous decline? The answer is an unequivocal *yes*. The human race generally has a long history of callous disregard of other life forms on the earth in favor of its own. An old but striking reminder of this indifference can be found in the accelerated extinction of a bird species in Audubon's time: the passenger pigeon. It is widely believed to be the most prolific bird ever to inhabit the planet. Audubon wrote of flocks of billions of the birds darkening the sky in flight. It was the most common bird in North America in the early nineteenth century. (One flock was measured to be a mile wide and *three hundred* miles long!)

A loss of habitat due to immigrant Europeans settling inland began their decline, but the primary cause originated with the commercialization of pigeon meat as a cheap food for the poor and for slaves, which resulted in hunting the birds on a massive scale. (Profits were there to be made, after all.) There was a slow decline in their numbers from 1800 to 1870, followed by a precipitous decline over the next thirty years. The last remaining bird died in the Cincinnati Zoo in 1914.

In a little over a hundred years, the most common, most populous bird on the planet was willfully removed from it by human greed and callousness and accomplished without the benefit of the killing methods later provided by the Industrial Revolution.

Fast forward to the present. Today, in our oceans alone, 90 percent of the big fish are gone. We have overfished the oceans to such a shocking extent that according to the United Nations' Food and Agricultural

Organization, the maximum wild-capture fisheries' potential from the world's oceans has probably been reached.

By 2050, the population of the earth will be *nine billion* people, most of them in developing countries. There is enough water for everyone, even in those numbers, except for the fact that it doesn't rain in the places where it is often needed the most.

There is no denying that even in America, a swollen population has created many demands and periodic corresponding shortages: oil, food, water, health care, social services, maintenance, and transportation, to name a few.

We need to take a hard look at how to curb further growth in our numbers and how to help other countries who are in far worse shape than we are. America must learn how to build an economy that is not based on population growth and consumerism. We also need to put the wealth of the world to work more effectively and efficiently to make the quality of life more comfortable for people of all levels of income. It is foolish and naïve of us to think that the problems of the rest of the world will not ultimately migrate to America.

Medical
26–21

Neuroendocrine Tumors

Neuroendocrine tumors develop among cells of the hormonal and nervous systems. They may be benign or malignant tumors. They are found most commonly in the intestine, but they also occur in the pancreas and in the rest of the body. The cells of these tumors share many common features, such as looking similar to each other, and they produce biogenic amines and polypeptide hormones.

If an NET has metastasized, and surgery has not been determined to create a probable cure, it can have a role in palliating the symptoms and increasing the lifespan of the patient. If long-term treatment with somatostatin analogs is prescribed, cholecystectomy is recommended to help ensure a positive outcome.

26–22

Alprazolam

Alprazolam is used to treat anxiety and panic disorders. It belongs to a class of medications called benzodiazepines, which act on the central nervous system to produce a calming effect. It enhances the effects of a certain natural chemical in the body, called gamma-aminobutyric acid.

Alprazolam is a controlled substance. It can cause paranoia or suicide, as well as impair memory, judgment, and/or coordination. It should not be combined with other substances, particularly alcohol, as it can slow breathing and even lead to a fatal outcome.

26–23

Corticobasal Degeneration

Corticobasal degeneration is often misdiagnosed as other conditions, including Parkinson's disease, but also as other neurological conditions, such as progressive supranuclear palsy, frontotemporal or Alzheimer's dementia, and primary aphasia.

CBD symptoms are typical in people fifty to seventy years of age. The disease usually lasts up to six years. A final diagnosis can only be made upon neuropathologic examination. Movement disorders and cortical dysfunctions associated with CBD include parkinsonism, alien hand syndrome, apraxia, and aphasia.

26–24

Acute Lymphoblastic Leukemia

Acute lymphoblastic leukemia is the most common type of cancer in children. It starts from white blood cells in the bone marrow, the soft inner part of bones. It develops from cells called lymphocytes, a white blood cell central to the immune system, or from lymphoblasts, an immature type of lymphocyte.

Acute lymphoblastic leukemia invades the blood and can spread throughout the body to other organs, such as the liver, spleen, and lymph nodes. But it does not normally produce tumors as do many types of cancer. It is an acute condition, which means it can progress quickly. Without treatment, it can be fatal within a few months.

Technical
26–25

Diodes

The diode is a solid-state device that will only permit current flow in one direction, or polarity, but not going in the opposite direction. It can be used as a protection device for DC-operated equipment. If equipment is connected accidentally to a battery with the wrong polarity, no damage would occur because no current would flow.

Diodes are very useful in power supplies to change AC voltage into pulsating DC voltage when used as a rectifier diode.

With the correct polarity, the voltage across a diode will let the current pass with no resistance or very easily. With the opposite polarity of voltage, the current will encounter a very high resistance, and current will not flow. When the current cannot pass through the diode, this is called *reverse bias*, but when the current can easily flow through the diode, this is referred to as *forward bias*.

26–26

Material Removal

Removing large material from machine parts has always been the job of powerful machine tools. Once a part has been machined, a finishing operation is usually required to perform small material removal to bring the part into tolerance of the specification.

At the present time, the finishing of parts is a manual operation. It is very time consuming, inconsistent, and prone to errors that can damage extensive parts beyond repair. A fan case can require eleven hours to finish by hand. Manual finishing can account for 10–20 percent of the total labor cost, and 10–30 percent of the manufactured parts need rework after the manual finishing process.

Audiobooks

The following is a brief list of book titles you can use as practice material. There could be many books available in the various audiobook categories within your own book collection. Moreover, many of the books listed below and others you may select for practice can be borrowed from your public library. The children's books are generally inexpensive to purchase, since many of them are very short and can be obtained online.

CHILDREN'S FICTION:

The Velveteen Rabbit by Margery Williams (published by Doubleday)

Page 13: "Near the house..." to Page 18: "...like these rabbits did."

The Secret Garden by Frances Hodgson Burnett (published by Millennium Publications)

Page 24: "She ran up the walk..." to Page 26: "...not telling the truth."

Dogzilla by Dav Pilkey (published by Harcourt Books) is recommended for a male reader.

Read the entire book.

The Dumb Bunnies by Dav Pilkey (published by Harcourt Books; used entire book) is recommended for a female reader.

Read the entire book.

Pinocchio by Carlo Collodi and translated by E. Harden (published by Puffin Books)

Chapter 1 (Great opening story)
Chapter 2 (Animated dialogue)
Chapter 3 (Geppeto fabricates Pinocchio)

BIOGRAPHICAL FICTION:

Lincoln by Gore Vidal (published by Vintage International)
Page 647: "A long row of carriages..." to Page 648: "...The president's been shot."

Fear of Flying by Erica Jong (published by Penguin Books)
Page 295: "I've noticed, anyway..." to Page 297: "...a rhythm all its own."

FICTION:

Call It Sleep by Henry Roth (published by the Noonday Press)
Page 29: "The table has been set..." to Page 33: "...in his father's presence..."
Page 151: "Here is a man..." to Page 155: "...would reveal the meaning." (Good dialogue)
Page 305: "The hours that had passed..." to Page 308: "...joyfully down the stairs."

ADULT FICTION WITH DIALOGUE:

The Escape by David Baldacci (published by Grand Central Publishing)
Chapter 2 in entirety
Page 195: "Fuller came out of the bathroom..." to Page 199: "Good night, Knox."

Finders Keepers by Stephen King (published by Scribner)
Page 27: "Morris grabbed a blanket..." to Page 29: "...never would have cried."

Page 234: "Statewide motorcycle..." to Page 241: "...find it somewhere else."

NONFICTION:

The Demon-Haunted World by Carl Sagan (published by Ballantine Books)
Page 107: "When a child tells..." to Page 108: "...or hallucinating, the same thing?"

Blink by Malcolm Gladwell (published by Little, Brown and Company)
Page 125: "A Crisis in the ER..." to Page 136: "...posted on the wall."
Page 248: "A Revolution in Classical Music..." to Page 252: "...from behind a screen."

Soul Mates by Thomas Moore (published by HarperCollins)
Page 3: "Attachment..." to Page 11: "...initiated, and deepened."
Page 211: "Insecurity..." to Page 215: "...find genuine courage."

BIOGRAPHICAL NONFICTION:

Genghis Khan by Jack Weatherford (published by Three Rivers Press) is recommended for a male reader.
Page 3: "Of the thousands of cities..." to Page 4: "...down the road of war."

Eleanor Roosevelt by Anjelina Michelle Keating (published by Pomegranate Communications, Inc.) is recommended for a female reader.
Pages 19 through 22

Sinatra: The Chairman by James Kaplan (published by Doubleday)
Page 14: "Doris Day had first gotten to know..." to Page 15: "...hours later than anyone else?"
Page 487: "With its brutal scenes of brainwashing..." to Page 489: "... from Turkey and southern Italy."

Autobiographical Nonfiction:

This Time Together by Carol Burnett (published by Harmony Books)
Early Days in Hollywood—entire chapter, Page 11
Stretching Pennies—entire chapter, Page 23
Rumplemayer's and the Mean Hostess—entire chapter, Page 41 (good dialogue)

Nonfiction:

The Informant by Kurt Eichenwald (published by Broadway Books)
Page 160: "The receptionist on duty…" to Page 161: "…commute was history."

Crook County by Nicole Gonzalez van Cleve (published by Stanford Law Books)
Page 91: "Fairness as a Dangerous Delusion…" to Page 92: "…I am the court record."
Page 148: "Bigotry and Abuse…" to Page 150: "…to describe him."

The Narcissist Next Door by Jeffrey Kluger (published by Riverhead Books)
Page 152: "The enduring dream…" to Page 153: "…it can't come too often."

Historical Nonfiction:

The March of Folly by Barbara Tuchman (published by Alfred A. Knopf)
Page 375: "In the illusion…" to Page 376: "…history is inexorable."

The Collected Essays, Journalism and Letters of George Orwell: Volume 4 In Front of Your Nose 1945–1950 (published by Harcourt, Brace, Jovanovich)
Page 136: "In our time…" to Page 137: "…a portion of one's brain."

Chapter Twenty-Seven
POTENTIAL AREAS OF WORK

This chapter outlines the varied areas of work offered by the voice over market, and some of the challenges those areas present to the voice actor.

Commercials

Commercials offer a great deal of acting range opportunities, as they are written in a variety of different moods and emotional levels. We often loosely express this in the terms *soft sell*, *medium sell*, and *hard sell*.

The following is a list of most of the general categories of commercial work:

Automotive	Internet
Retail	Retail/Malls
Travel/Hospitality	Services
Business/Corporate	The Arts
Banks/Financial	Restaurants
Public Service Announcements	Medical/Hospitals

Narrations

- Tell a story or relate an experience
- Show and tell, describe
- Teach, instruct, inform

- Endorse a product, company, service, or philosophy
- Praise or criticize

Narrations are acted out on a generally moderate emotional level, sometimes with intense focus, especially with certain documentaries.

The following is a list of most of the general categories of narration work:

Business/Corporate	Medical/Technical
Documentary/Historical	Theatrical
Biographical	Psychological
General Interest	Scientific
Human Interest	Travel
Explainer Videos (a huge market)	Learning/training

Medical and Technical

Medical and *technical* are very specific areas that require an ability to pronounce words that are difficult to pronounce with smoothness and ease. Medical and technical are categories for which doing a separate demo is justified. This is a particularly good area of business potential for women, as there is great demand for women's voices by medical media producers and hospitals. In addition, women are often used for long medical or technical scripts, sometimes singly, or alternating with men's voices, to give variety to a long script.

Audiobooks

Audiobooks are more popular than ever. Almost all authors with new books routinely want to create an audiobook version. Audiobooks are very useful for the listener who may be on a trip in the car or on an airplane, and listening to a book helps to pass the time and eliminate the tedium of travel.

The general categories of audiobooks are outlined as follows:

Fiction	Nonfiction
Children's books 5–8	Biographical
(Early readers)	Historical
Children's books 8–12	Political commentary
(Middle grade)	Social commentary
Children's books 12–14 and up	Self-help
(Young teens)	Inspirational
Adult fiction	
Historical fiction	

Some people have exceptional voices for children's books, both for telling the story and playing the various characters in the book convincingly. The *Harry Potter* series is a standout example of this phenomenon.

Audiobooks are very time consuming in three areas: preparation, recording, and editing. The average book is around three hundred pages. The recording time for a three-hundred-page book is about two and a half to three six-hour days, assuming two three-hour sessions a day, with a two-hour lunch break and a twenty-minute break in each of the three-hour sessions. Preparation time is almost directly tied to the difficulty of the script. Editing time is generally equal to the recording time or longer. If you are or become a killer audio editor, you will learn ways to shorten that time considerably.

Politicals

Political spots are very big in the United States, particularly in view of the continuing emergence of political action groups in both political parties over the last thirty or so years. The media buys are off the charts.

If you possess an acutely persuasive delivery style, you can probably pick up a lot of political work. Keep in mind that in this day and age, the respective parties want you to be a registered member of their political camps. If you're a Democrat, don't expect to work for Republicans, and vice versa. Their perception is that you need to be a disciple to deliver the message with conviction.

Being the voice for a political campaign can be very lucrative, especially with the huge budgets of today's political campaigns.

Broadcast Imaging

Most of the station-break announcements that promote radio or TV stations or their programs are done not by staff on-air talents but by freelancers working in their home studios. The studios send them sets of scripts once or twice a week, and they record, edit, and return them to the station, usually on WAV files. The station then organizes and programs them into its automation to play at the scheduled times.

The vast majority of voice talents who do broadcast imaging work have a strong broadcast background as DJs, announcers, or anchors.

Characters/Dialects/Accents

For people who have the talent and ability to do this work, this is a most interesting and fun realm of the business. Some people have a knack for off-the-wall, nutty, unusual characters. Others have an exceptional feel for dialects or accents. Let's look at how dialects and accents are defined:

Dialect—a particular form of language that is peculiar to a specific region or social group; a category of language that stands apart in vocabulary and grammar, as well as articulation. It is generally spoken by people bound by geography or class. When a language and its articulation become a standard for a body of people (such as the general population of a country), any pronunciation that deviates from this standard we may define as an *accent*.

"The book is written in the dialect of Cajun Louisiana."

Accent—a distinctive mode of pronunciation of a language, especially one associated with a particular nation, locality, or social class.

"The man was immediately identifiable as a Russian because of his strong accent."

With dialects and accents, you must be absolutely authentic. There are a number of books that are accompanied by CDs that you can use to refine your own dialects and accents. These are listed in the next section, "Recommended Reading," at the end of this book.

You can best work on characters by recording the sources you want to emulate and working on and refining your imitations diligently. Record and listen to yourself as you go.

Messages on Hold

Messages on hold is a relatively easy area of business to farm and grow. Many businesses use messages on the phone to alleviate boredom in the person on hold; tell news of progress by the company; and promote new products, services, or special offers.

Some of my students have selected office buildings in the downtown areas where they live, poring over the directory and cold calling or simply showing up at offices to make a pitch. (I recommend calling first.) As you build your client base, add each client to your customer portfolio to use in your presentations to new potential clients. Put together a short demo (sixty seconds) of four or five segments of different companies with your voice and a different music background for each segment. You can get some seminal ideas from the Internet. Just google *Messages on Hold*. It's important to put your own stamp of creativity on this, since the potential is to get paid not only for the voice over work but also for creating the script materials if you are a decent writer. Writing *and* narrating can *double* your fees.

Recommended Reading

On Language

- *Essential English Grammar* by Philip A. Gucker (published by Dover Publications)

  My favorite book on grammar. It cuts to the chase without getting too academic.

- *Grammar Smart* by the Princeton Review (published by Random House)

  Similar to the above. A bit more detailed.

- *Voice and Articulation* by Kenneth Crannell (published by Cengage Learning)

  One of the definitive books on articulation. Filled with numerous and varied exercises.

- *Speaking Clearly* by Jeffrey Hahner, Martin Sokoloff, and Sandra Salisch (published by Waveland Press, Inc.; includes practice CD-ROM)

  Written primarily for speech, it contains many ear-training exercises that help monitor and correct speech patterns, with an examination of the root causes of anxiety.

- *Fundamentals of Voice & Diction* by Lyle V. Mayer (published by Brown & Benchmark)

Filled with interesting and amusing exercises and lively practice material, this is a go-to manual for voice and diction.

- *The Articulate Voice: An Introduction to Voice and Diction* by Lynn K. Wells (published by Pearson)

Clearly and concisely delivers the how tos on voice production and the improvement of skills with pitch, pace, volume, and timbre.

Accents and Dialects

- *Accents and Dialects for Stage and Screen* by Paul Meier (published by Paul Meier Dialect Services)

This in-depth book by one of the best dialect coaches in America comprehensively delineates twenty-four accents and comes with twelve practice CDs. A must-have.

Dialects covered are as follows: Afrikaans (South Africa), American Deep South (Mississippi/Georgia/Alabama), American Southern (Kentucky/Tennessee), Australian, Cockney, Down East New England, French, General American, German, Hampshire, Indian, Irish, Italian, Liverpool, New York, Northern Ireland, Russian, Scottish, South Boston, Spanish (Castilian and Colonial), Standard British English (Received Pronunciation), Welsh, Yiddish, and Yorkshire.

On the twelve accompanying CDs (each containing two dialects/accents), Paul Meier speaks the entire text. You hear him demonstrate, in dialect, the signature sounds in isolation, the word lists, the practice sentences, and the monologues. For each dialect/accent, there are eight CD tracks corresponding to the eight chapter sections, making it easy to select the track of your choice. Total running time of each CD is about sixty minutes.

- *Accents: A Manual for Actors* by Robert Blumenfeld (published by Proscenium Publishers, Inc.; includes online practice audio)

  This practical reference manual, with its precise instructions on how to master over one hundred accents and dialects, has established itself as one of the most comprehensive guidebooks available. Order with CDs or online audio.

- *Classically Speaking: Dialects for Actors* by Patricia Fletcher (published by lulu.com)

  This is an excellent book by one of the most respected voice, speech, dialogue, and dialect coaches in theater and film.

- *How to Do Accents* by Edda Sharpe and Jan Haydn Rowles (published by Oberon Books; accents include neutral American, classical American, mid-Atlantic, and standard British; with practice CD and audio downloads)

  Another essential tool for stage and voice over actors. It helps you analyze your own voice and learn to break it down into component sounds to replicate the vowels and consonants of specific accents.

- *Teach Yourself Accents: Europe* by Robert Blumenfeld (published by Limelight Editions; includes practice CD)

  This series is aimed at young actors who are new to accent study.

- *Teach Yourself Accents: The British* by Robert Blumenfeld (published by Limelight Editions; includes practice CD)

- *Teach Yourself Accents: North America* by Robert Blumenfeld (published by Limelight Editions; includes practice CD)

- *Stage Dialects* by Jerry Blunt (published by the Dramatic Publishing Company)

Considered the definitive work on the subject in the theater, it covers Brooklyn, American Southern, Japanese, Cockney, Irish, Scottish, French, Italian, German, and Russian, among others.

Standard English Accent

- *How to Do Standard English Accents* by Sharpe & Rowles (published by Oberon Books)

  (Part One—Neutral standard English accent)

  (Part Two—Upper- and upper-middle-class varieties of standard English accent)

  A thorough examination of English accents, it includes free downloads of exercises and sample sentences of standard English accents.

Voice Health

- *The Voice Book: Caring For, Protecting, and Improving Your Voice* by Kate DeVore and Starr Cookman (published by Chicago Review Press)

  The most complete book out there on voice health.

On Voice Over

- *There's Money Where Your Mouth Is* by Elaine A. Clark (published by Allworth Press)

  The first consequential book on voice over; now available in its second edition and printing. A must-have.

- *VO: Tales and Techniques of a Voice-Over Actor* by Harlan Hogan (published by Allworth Press)

  A delightful book, crammed with lots of interpretive gems.

- *Voice Actor's Guide to Recording at Home and On the Road* by Harlan Hogan and Jeffrey Fisher (published by Cengage Learning)

  The first book on selecting and working with your own gear.

- *The Art of Voice Acting* by James R. Alburger (published by Focal Press)

  A good mix of technique, tutelage, and the business side of voice overs.

- *Voice for Hire* by Randy Thomas (published by Crown Publishing Group)

  An insightful book about the business from the voice of the Oscars.

- *Voiceovers: Everything You Need to Know about How to Make Money with Your Voice* by Terri Apple (published by Michael Wiese Productions)

  A diverse book filled with tools, tips, and great interviews.

- *Voice-Over Voice Actor: What It's Like Behind the Mic* by Yuri Lowenthal and Tara Platt (published by Bug Bot Press)

  Filled with twenty anecdotes from VO professionals.

- *More Than Just a Voice: The REAL Secret to Voiceover Success* by Dave Courvoisier (published by NomSayn Enterprises)

  This is a very popular book on just about every aspect of the voice over business, with plenty of new ideas and great tips.

- *How to Read Copy* by Adrian Cronauer (published by Bonus Books)

  I like this book. It was written way back in the late '80s by a Vietnam veteran about whom the movie *Good Morning Vietnam* was made. An amazing amount of wisdom in its pages. You'll need to find one on the used-book market, as it has been out of print for some time. It originally came with a cassette with exercises and examples.

On Acting

- *Respect for Acting* by Uta Hagen (published by Wiley)

  The ultimate modern treatise on acting by a consummate coach, whose students include Geraldine Page, Fritz Weaver, Jack Lemmon, and Jason Robards, to name a few. A most revealing, interesting, and informative book.

- *Acting in Film* by Michael Caine (published by Applause Theatre & Cinema Books)

  A wonderful book on film acting, which I have included in this list because voice over delivery has many similarities to film acting. A superb book about how to get into character.

On the English Language

- *Crazy English* by Richard Lederer (published by Pocket Books)

  This is a book for those English-language lovers who enjoy a good-humored observation of the peculiarities of the English language.

  Here's a tantalizing excerpt from the book:

  "You have to marvel at the unique lunacy of the English language, in which your house can simultaneously burn up and burn down, in which you can fill in a form by filling out a form, in which you can add up a column of figures by adding them down, in which your alarm clock goes off by going on, in which you can be inoculated for measles by being inoculated against measles, and in which you first chop a tree down—and then you chop it up."

Eats, Shoots and Leaves by Lynne Truss (published by Gotham Books)

Another inventive and imaginative book about the language—this one about *punctuation*.

A couple of passages from the book:

"A woman, without her man, is nothing."

"A woman: without her, man is nothing."

On Motivation

- *Do What You Love, The Money Will Follow* by Marsha Sinetar (published by Dell Publishing)

  One of my very favorite books. The number-one reason for choosing a voice over career should be the joy and passion you derive from doing the work, and that primary motivation is what this book is all about.

Epilogue

Finally, here are several quotes from famous and successful people for you to ponder as you consider spending your time and resources pursuing a career in voice over. I hope they will further inspire you.

It's never too late to be who you might have been.

—George Eliot (1819–1880),Writer

Either you decide to stay in the shallow end of the pool or you go out in the ocean.

—Christopher Reeve (1952–2004), Actor

When you reach for the stars you may not quite get one, but you won't come up with a handful of mud either.

—Leo Burnett (1891–1971)
Advertising Executive

I can't conceive of a more rewarding and fulfilling way to make a living than doing voice over work. It is uncommonly interesting and challenging, and you can now do it from the comfort of your home studio. You can also market to the world from there.

If you're entirely new to this discipline, don't make the mistake of assuming that compliments about your voice from several people offer you an automatic entry into the voice over world. Over the years, I have had a few students who mistakenly assumed that with a great voice and minimal training, they were assured a successful career doing voice over work. Nothing could be further from the truth.

Voice over work presents many challenges. This book has addressed those that deal with doing the work itself. There are also marketing challenges, which are dealt with in other books about voice over (see "Recommended Reading").

You must understand that learning how to do this is a *process*. Everyone with whom I have worked has come to the table with some linguistic or interpretive habits that must be addressed and fixed. Changing habits takes time—and *persistence*. It is not unusual for me to remind a student about a particular issue countless times before it sinks in and the long-ingrained habit disappears.

I have also observed in these many years of coaching that a little humility goes a long way in the learning process.

Here is a great story about the good things that can happen to those who patiently persevere:

One of my most successful former students originally came to me from a career in the construction business that had come to an abrupt halt during the recession of 2008, leaving him high and dry. He had a gorgeous bass-baritone voice, a high-school education with a below-average English curriculum, and a real passion for learning how to interpret and perform scripts.

We had a lot of linguistic catching up to do. He prepared diligently for the coaching sessions and performed very well on his first demos of commercials and narrations. In his first year, he did almost two hundred fifty auditions for work online. He landed two jobs. The next year, he did almost three hundred auditions and landed four jobs. The third year was pivotal. Twenty-plus projects. The fourth year, he doubled his client base. At the initial publication date of this book, he has done over a hundred projects in that year and was still adding more clients. An agent from Atlanta called *him* and told him he wanted to be his agent for the greater Atlanta market. That almost never happens. Most voice over actors go hunting for agents themselves.

As this tale demonstrates, hard work, patience, and determination do pay off in the end, but it takes time. Harlan Hogan calls it "the Long Haul." Starting and growing any business takes time and patience, and the voice over market is no exception. You must be patient with both the learning and the marketing process.

The potential to earn a substantial income is also a strong motivator, although as you can observe from the previous story, the first two or three years in the market are probably going to produce minimal financial rewards. Then again, you may get lucky and land four or five solid repeat clients. It happens. I just don't want you to count on it. Prepare for the long haul, and take disappointment in your stride. Rejection is a huge part of this business, no matter how good you are.

Interestingly, another student of mine went from zero to a six-figure income at the end of her first year. She is the only one among my students who has achieved that level of income up to this point in time. She was doggedly determined to do this, and very persistent.

While you're out there marketing to the world, continue to endeavor to learn all you can and work hard to become the best you can be. I've had too many students who finished training with me, focused exclusively on marketing themselves, and stopped practicing. The best people with whom I've worked in this business *always* put in a continuing effort to refine their craft.

If you want to make your mark in this business, I hope you can appreciate from what you have read in these pages that you need to learn as much about the English language as you possibly can. Learn how to apply that knowledge to the interpretation of every script you encounter. To that end, it is my wish that this book will be a significant tutor and motivator for your continuing development.

John Burr
June 2022

Index

Made in the USA
Middletown, DE
14 October 2023

40804277R00156